The Spiritual Warrior:

An Interdimensional Technique Manual

by
Shakura Rei

The Spiritual Warrior:
An Interdimensional Technique Manual
By Shakura Rei

©

United States Copyright, 1997
Sunstar Publishing, Ltd.
116 North Court Street
Fairfield, Iowa

Cover Design: Therese Cross

Library of Congress Catalog Card Number: 97–065709
ISBN 1-887472-28-2

Readers interested in obtaining further information on the
subject matter of this book are invited to correspond with
The Secretary, Sunstar Publishing, Ltd.
116 North Court Street, Fairfield, Iowa 52556

ACKNOWLEDGMENTS

I would like to honor my friends and co-creators from the Ashtar Command who, with patience and love, have guided me, screaming and kicking through this life's experiences. They said my healing techniques needed to be brought to the public and asked me to write this book.

I honor and bless all interdimensional beings of Light, especially Archangel Michael, Kuthumi, and the various ascended Masters who have helped me and educated me in more ways than I can mention.

To my soul mate, Bob Schlein, for his healing hands, his encouragement and his constant support, I give my deepest love.

I wish to acknowledge my friends who refused to let me give up on this book when I had reached wit's end, and who helped, and sometimes carried me, through my most difficult times. I also honor the gentle San Lira for his contribution to the artwork and for his encouragement; Elaine DeVore for her wealth of astrological knowledge and her willingness to share it with me; my editors; the people who shared their computers and computer knowledge with me; little Nahied, our "space kitty," for the humor and love she constantly stirs within me; and the most beautiful and loving four-legged "best friend" that I have ever known, Naomi, who at fifteen years old passed over as I was writing this book.

DEDICATION

I dedicate this manual to Mother Earth who has suffered, endured and rejoiced over her human inhabitants, and to the numerous intergalactic servers on Earth and in the skies who have dedicated themselves to her healing and to the future survival of the human species.

TABLE OF CONTENTS

Introduction...7
Part I: A First Day..9
    Sleeping 10
    Awakening 28
From Out the Turbulent Waters 40
Part II: The Spiritual Warrior...43
Ascension Tansmutation 44
Rays and Attunements 61
    The Transmutational Light Beam 63
    Rainbow Warrior Attunement 64
    Kwan Yin Attunement and Healing 64
    Kwan Yin's Magnified Healing 65
    Reiki I, II and Master...65
    The Master Reiki Ray 65
Understanding Consciousness..68
    Description of Various Forms of Intelligence 72
        Creatures 72
        Negative Thought Forms and Thought Form Monsters.................72
        Astral Monster Projectiles 73
        Implants...73
        Devices 73
        Mind/Soul Fragments or "Soul Retrieval"................73
        Extraterrestrials 74
        Discarnate Earthbound Entities or "Ghosts" 74
        Angels, Dark and Light 77
        The Dark Angels or "Dark Forces".............................77
        The Light Angels...77
Part III: The Technique 81
Protection 83
Cellular Memory Release...85
Release of Undesirable and Parasitic Energies 91
    Release of Creatures 91
    Release of Negative Thought Forms...................................92
    Release of Thought Form Monsters and Astral Monster
        Projectiles 92

Removal of Implants and Devices 93
Integrating Mind/Soul Fragments or "Soul Retrieval" 94
Release of Earthbound Discarnates..95
Release of the Dark Forces..98
Clearing Houses and Buildings 106
Healing Children 107
Healing Animals..107
Releasing Land..108
Clearing Mechanical Things 109
Releasing Food 110
Healing the Bodies, Aura and Chakras..112
Repairing Auric Holes and Rips...113
Opening the Chakras..113
Resonating and Fluffing the Aura 116
Putting It Together..118
Part IV: Conclusion 121
Case Studies 123
Illustrations ....
The Master Glands...133
Organs of Digestive System 134
Organs of Voice and Respiration 135
The Male Reproductive System...136
The Female Reproductive System 137
The Chakras
— before opening 138
— after opening 139
Suggested Reading and References...140

INTRODUCTION

**...Two roads diverged in a wood, and I —
I took the one less traveled by,
And that has made all the difference.**

— Robert Frost, *The Road Not Taken*

This small book came about at the request of my spiritual guidance. I have to admit that when asked to compile this information and present it to the public, I had serious reservations. My work is rather esoteric, and I have met less than a handful of people who are courageous enough, or even have the desire, to work within these realms. But I was informed that people's reservations are not so much due to a lack of courage, as due to a lack of understanding. The other realms are an unknown to most, and is the unknown not a scary thing? Truly there are few among us who are willing to take the first step into the unfamiliar and forge a pathway for others to follow and build upon. Myself and a few others have taken that step.

It is my sincerest wish that the information in this book be of benefit to all readers, whether they utilize the techniques or not. One need not be clairvoyant or psychic to benefit from the wealth of information contained in this book. Some advanced skills are useful if one wishes to employ *all* the methods described, but I expect the reader to choose those which best serve her purpose.

This book is divided into three parts. Part I is autobiographical. I hope that the reader may relate to some of my experiences, or at least recognize that boundless possibilities may arise from even the most difficult circumstances.

Part II elaborates on the concept of co-creation with all consciousness, seen and unseen, and our role within it. This part also describes the types of beings found within the other realms, and the ways in which they may aid or harm us. None of us are immune to these cosmic forces and principles, no matter what our purpose or service; therefore a thorough understanding will greatly assist us on our life's journey.

The third and last part of this book is an instruction manual of inter-dimensional healing techniques that have been refined through years of experimentation and direct teachings from the Masters and angelic realms.

This book is meant to be read from beginning to end (not as some do, from back to front, or in pieces). It is absolutely vital that the techniques in Part III not be employed without a thorough understanding of the concepts put forth in Part II. A wrong attitude or approach, especially when dealing with Dark Forces, could create a very unpleasant lesson, instead of a rewarding healing for the client!

The use of the third person pronoun in written text remains an ongoing dilemma, therefore the pronouns he/she and him/her have been used randomly and without any intention of gender bias.

Cosmic law states that no one may take away another's soul lessons nor consciously attempt to correct another's painful conditions without that one's permission. As spiritual healers, this places many of us uncomfortably close to a rather fine line. Due to the rapidly evolving "new human" and ascension of this planet, the resolution of human karma, on a personal and global level, is now appropriate. Grace from the higher realms has been extended to all of Earth and negative karma is now being absolved. At this point, however, it must be understood that this is neither absolute nor complete, nor does it instantaneously apply to every person. As healers we must honor an individual's experiences and allow them to continue if that is still appropriate. The techniques involving Cellular Memory Release and Dark Force attachment release, clearly remove karma. Because of the depth of this work, and as most of the work is done remotely, permission must always be granted from the higher Self of the individual being released. The profound degree of healing that frequently takes place through these techniques may well evoke a great temptation to release loved ones, unbeknownst to them, who would never give their conscious permission. To perform a healing on such a person under those circumstances, may put one at risk of accruing a new karmic debt for attempting to release the karma of another. Please, use your common sense, follow your intuition and listen to your guidance in all matters.

An absolute dedication to serving the Light is a prerequisite for this work. If any of these techniques are used with the purpose of harming in any way, remember the cosmic principle just mentioned … one reaps that which one has sown.

If this book can assist you in attaining your spiritual goals, then I am indeed blessed.

May the Light of the higher realms comfort and support you.

Shakura Rei

PART I

A FIRST DAY

...And God brought about a division between
the light and the darkness.
And God began calling the light Day,
but the darkness he called Night.
And there came to be evening
and there came to be morning,
a first day.

— The Holy Scriptures, *Genesis I: 4-5*

SLEEPING

When I beheld all these things, I cried out in pain,
Oh Daughter of Zeus, is this indeed the Earth? Is this Man?"
In a soft and anguished voice she replied,
"What you see is the Soul's path, and it is paved
with sharp stones and carpeted with thorns.
This is only the shadow of Man. This is Night.
But wait! Morning will soon be here!"

— Kahlil Gibran, *The Voice of the Master*

My life began in Giessen Wieseck, Germany, in 1951, as the illegitimate daughter of a seventeen-year-old German war orphan. My mother had been taken in by a farm family during her last months of pregnancy. After ten hours of labor assisted by a midwife, I arrived in the world in my mother's bed. Three months later we left the kindly farmers and came under the abusive care of my natural father. When I was two-and-a-half years old he deserted my mother and kidnapped me, leaving me with a family that he knew. My mother resigned herself to this, as she had no way of taking care of herself, let alone a child. Here begin my memories. The stairs I was carried up on the way to my bedroom. The gloomy room. The crib against the wall. The circles and spirals that appeared on the wall and grew bigger and bigger until I screamed in fear that they would engulf me.

Six months later, on the day of my third birthday, my mother, starving and with no hope for the future, was making plans for our demise. She was going to pick me up the next day and jump into the river with me in her arms, drowning us both. As she was formulating her plans, an American airman noticed the depth of her agitation and asked if he could be of help. This immediately kindled a relationship between the two. The next day my mother delivered me from the couple with whom I was staying, and the three of us attempted to become a family. We moved to France where we lingered for a year while waiting for Mom's legal paperwork to be processed before they could be married and we were permitted to come to the U.S. They married. I was adopted. At five years old, I took my first step on American soil.

School proved to be a disaster. My mother spoke to me in German, French and broken English; my father spoke English and broken German. I had too many accents. By the time I entered second grade I still wasn't speaking English correctly. Consequently, I was placed in a special speech class. I remember speaking in front of a candle and practicing my "s" and "th" for the teacher. All of us who went to the speech class were considered stupid by the other kids. The consensus seemed to be that if you couldn't speak correctly, you must be an idiot. I was one of the idiots. I loathed school and was miserable around the crowds of people. The other children's interactions with each other were fun and playful, but I didn't know what to say to them or how to respond. I was sorely lacking in social skills, so I isolated myself and spent my free time playing hopscotch and jacks by myself, or running the circumference of the playground. I would have been one of the fastest runners if I hadn't spent so much time picking myself up from the ground. My speed was good, but I was constantly tripping over my feet, falling down and skinning my knees. During the time at this school I developed an uncontrollable bowel disorder which lasted for months and brought me great ridicule and embarrassment. The doctors could find nothing wrong with me and suggested I see a child psychologist. The psychologist spoke to my parents and then to me. Shortly after our discussion my disorder subsided, but was replaced by a sudden weight gain of fifteen pounds.

My only refuge was to be alone. Fortunately that was not difficult to do, as we lived in the country, the only house for a mile in three directions. Across the road was a walnut grove, behind the house stretched a field of wild watermelons. Dry dirt, rattlesnakes and jack rabbits inhabited the other two sides. My mother took in any stray animals we came across, and soon we had more cats and their litters living under the house than we could keep track of. We also raised turkeys, chickens and a stray dog that she had found. These animals were the closest things to friends that I had.

Behind the house lay a fallen tree, its horizontal trunk just close enough to the ground for me to climb on and straddle. As I sat on the trunk I could make it bounce, so I pretended to be a cowboy riding the range. Me and my horse ... herding the chickens.

I enjoyed roaming the fields and hunting for chicken eggs, even though they were usually rotten by the time I found them. I would often climb the tree and sit next to the rooster at twilight as he crowed the ending of a day. Across the road, in the walnut grove, I would wander and feel peace. It was pretty there. I pretended to be back in the forest in France, where we had lived. The soil in the grove was rich, not dry and hard like the fields around our house, and I found comfort among the trees; they were safe. I felt a need to be protected from the world — what little I had experienced of it — for at that time the world felt very threatening and cruel. I would sit for hours in the walnut grove, digging tunnels in the soil with my mother's kitchen spoons.

It never occurred to me to wonder what my parents did with the chickens and turkeys they raised. I knew we ate chicken and turkey, but in my mind, what was served on the table was not the same thing as what ran around our yard. I would watch my mother pull the feathers from the chickens and gag at the hideous stench as she immersed them in a pot of boiling water. Where did she get those horrible, smelly things? Somehow, Dad produced them in the backyard, behind some bushes where I was not permitted to go.

One day I decided to find out. I had been told not to go in the backyard for a while, but I went anyway and snuck up on my father just as he had cut off a chicken's head. The head was thrown in a hole in the ground, and the chicken was running around headless. I screamed! It was the most horrible thing I could imagine. I ran into my room and hid, crying.

My father's family, who lived in a neighboring town, was also of no general support or comfort to me. He had four brothers and four sisters. His father had died and his mother lived in an old ramshackle house without plumbing. To get to her house from the road, we had to walk across a little stream on a make-shift bridge built of two two-by-fours. It always scared me to walk across that plank. I thought if I fell I might drown in the stream, though there was less than a foot of water in it. None of my dad's family really cared for Mom or me. His sisters carried a controlled hostility towards us, but his brothers and mother were a little more tolerant. I was uncomfortable around all of them except Dad's youngest brother who gave me the most attention. One day he even rounded up Grandma's steer, put me on his back and led me around the yard. I had seen the steer in the pasture and was fascinated with him. I wanted to make friends with the animal, but he never came near me, and I was warned not to go in the pasture with him. I was not used to much kindness or attention, and it was thrilling to sit on a real animal's back — far better than the fallen trunk I rode.

One day, apparently a special occasion, the whole family got together at Grandma's. The brothers were outside in the yard carrying on over something. From a distance I looked around to see what was happening and saw them butchering the steer. Blood was spattered everywhere, and they were cutting a chunk out of its side. The horror of the sight swelled in my body, searing my emotions and curdling my stomach. It was too revolting. I hid in the field until I heard my mother call me for dinner. Grandma had cooked a roast from the recently butchered steer. I left the table and vomited. And vomited. And vomited.

By this time my parents were in their mid-twenties. They had both been poor and times had been difficult for them. Considering their past, they tried to raise me to the best of their abilities, but they had so many of their own personal problems that mine seemed insignificant. I never spoke to them. I never spoke to anyone.

Though my parents never argued in front of me, when they thought that I was asleep or not around, they would yell at each other. I was convinced that it was about me. What else could it be about? There was something wrong with me. The proof was that no one liked me; I had no friends. I took to walking in our rattlesnake-infested fields and asked the snakes to bite me. They never did. I could find no happiness in life nor peace in death.

When I was nine I was told we were moving to England. Good! Anyplace was better than America. Maybe the English people were kinder. Maybe I would make a friend. However, the three years we spent in England turned out to be the worst years of my life. Though my father was in the military, we never lived in military housing, but rather with the people of the country. I was sent to an American school, and I loathed it! My German heritage was ridiculed. I was taller than any boy in class, frizzy-haired and homely. Although I quickly lost the weight, until I did I was "Fatty" to many of my school peers. I didn't understand what I'd done to deserve such cruelty, nor why I should feel so much pain. I spent most recesses alone at the far side of the playground or hiding in a bathroom stall crying. The feelings of unworthiness, loneliness and grief stayed with me like a smoldering fire.

At the age of nine I was pretty much on my own getting to and from school. I had to catch a public bus several blocks from my house to the train station, after which I rode over an hour on a military bus. The hour ride was torture! The favorite pastime among the other children was to tell horror stories to which I was extremely sensitive. My sensitivity spurred them on even more. They knew that by the time we arrived back at the train station in the late afternoon, I had yet another bus ride and then a long walk home. In the winter I would walk home in the dark. Being cruel, as children can be, they told me the most graphic, horrible tales of evil men who murdered and ate people. The more afraid I became, the more gruesome their stories became. Filled with terror, I would run past the houses in the dark for fear an evil being would grab, kill, and eat me.

I also had a constant fear of missing my public bus, which I did on several occasions. More than once the bus would come to the end of the line, with me, the only one left, lost and crying. I would be taken to the police station to wait until my father came to pick me up. Missing the bus and not arriving home on time was always very traumatic, especially for my mother, as we had no telephone. The only phones were at the local businesses, and not all of them had one. We only had one car which my father took to work. Because of timing, he was unable to drive me to any of my various stops, or see me onto the bus.

One particular late afternoon, as I arrived at the train station to catch my public bus for home, I stepped into a tremendous storm. There was torrential rain, ankle-high water, and lightning crashing all around me. As I went to wait for my bus, I realized that my bus fare was missing from my lunch pail. I knew it had been stolen. Next to the bus stop was a candy store, owned and run by a woman from whom I frequently bought bubble gum in the morning. I went into her shop, escaping the storm, and asked her if she would loan me bus fare — I would pay her back in the morning. She ordered me out of her store. I reminded her who I was, that she saw me at the bus stop every day and that I would certainly repay her in the morning. She said she would not tolerate a beggar or loiterer. She would not give me a cent and virtually threw me out. The train station was packed with everyone huddled under the covered bus stop. I tried to squeeze in, but there was no room for me, so I stood outside in the storm, cold, scared and crying. People hurried by, but no one seemed to care about or even notice me. I couldn't understand it. There must be something terribly wrong with me, or she surely would have loaned me the money. I believed myself to be horribly different and thought of the rattlesnakes. I had made myself so available to be bitten. Why hadn't they done it?

I heard my name called. A man who rode the bus with me in the mornings was on his way home from work. Whatever was I doing here in the rain? I should have been home long ago. I mustered up all the courage I could and asked if he would please loan me bus fare, explaining to him what had happened. He listened, understanding and sympathetic. He put his arm around me and assured me that not only would he loan me bus fare, but he would see me home and explain to my mother what had happened. Many years later, as an adult practicing spiritual healing, I reached deep within myself and forgave the woman at the candy store and projected my heartfelt love and thanks for the kindness the gentleman had shown me. It was a rare kindness for me, and one never to be forgotten.

I found England miserable. The houses that we lived in were made of cold stone. I was always chilled to my bones. The sun rarely shone and it seemed as if it would never stop raining. Not surprisingly, my nightmares started in England. Something was always after me. I would run through buildings looking for someplace to hide. Sometimes I would go to the basement of the building and find hideous monsters locked in cages, or I would try to fly away, but could never get far from the monster's reach.

We went back to Germany for a short time, where I stayed with my mother's brother and family. They lived in the outskirts of a village surrounded by woods and meadow. The sun shone and the air was dry. I played with my cousins, ate homemade butter, cheese and bread, and slept in a feather bed. It was heaven!

But then, back to the gloom of England.

The one good thing about England was that my parents had sent me to riding school, The Loudwater Riding Academy. We went to London and bought me jodhpur boots, pants and hat, as the academy required "proper dress." I also needed a riding jacket, but my parents had already spent more than they could afford, so instead, my mother knitted me a tan sweater. On the front were two horse heads facing each other, one brown and the other beige. The academy permitted me this slight transgression from the dress code. I was in such bliss being around horses and learning to ride that I didn't care that everyone else wore jodhpur boots up to the knees and mine only went to the ankle, or that they looked dashing in their riding jackets, while I wore a home-knitted sweater. Come rain or shine, once a week I rode through the meadows of England.

There was a horse at the academy named Monty — a large palomino gelding who was considered to have a mean streak. The students all dreaded when he was assigned to them as their mount. Even the "toughest" boy at the academy was scared every time he had to groom or clean Monty's stall. I, being the newest equestrian, was directed not to go near him. What rubbish, I thought. I observed Monty and decided he was an unhappy animal who merely needed love and kindness. When no one was around, I went into his stall, speaking gently. Laying his ears back, he turned his head to see who had entered. I continued to talk as I walked to his head. Monty looked at me with curiosity and slowly brought his ears forward. Calmly, I reached to pet him, and instead of his usual bite, he permitted me to put my arms around his great neck. I was so happy! We were kindred spirits, Monty and I — both misunderstood and both disliked. But Monty was past his middle age and had grown resentful and angry. I was still young. It hurt my heart to see what had happened to him, and I feared it would happen to me. I told the academy that I was not afraid of the big palomino, and when they saw that I was the only rider he didn't buck, roll off or bite, they permitted me to be around him. Whenever he wasn't being ridden and I had free time, I would sit on the straw in his stall and we would silently communicate. I felt good around him and I knew he more than tolerated me — he liked me!

The academy gave me a glimmer of hope in my young life. I had progressed through advanced riding to intermediate jumping. I loved it! I was going to become a champion rider and enter steeplechase. Another National Velvet, even! Why not? What could stop me?

Ah, the folly of hope. My parents informed me that we were going back to the U.S. My academy days were over. We moved to southern California this time. No trees. No green grass. Just desert, smog and people.

The next four years found me coming out of my shell a little bit. After all, I had puberty and boys to contend with. At school I made one or two friends and desperately hoped they would remain such. It was futile, though. They invariably found other girlfriends who were more fun than me, and soon they stopped seeing me altogether. So what was fun? I was the last to know. Ask me about serious — that I knew. The boy/girl game was interesting, but shallow, although I seemed to be the only one that knew it. I wore the game out and soon lost interest. School was, as usual, awful. I had become so self-conscious and insecure by then, that the social life of a young teen was more than I could handle emotionally. Not that I had to worry, as no one invited me to anything anyway. But to make sure they didn't, I isolated myself even more.

In England I had discovered the wonderful joy of reading and devoured books. My reading progressed from books such as *The Black Stallion* to the writings of John Steinbeck, Somerset Maugham, Tennessee Williams and Eugene O'Neill. These authors depicted the strengths and frailties of the human spirit and helped me to see that I wasn't alone. These and other authors gave me a canvas upon which I painted my own suffering, and with each brush stroke the pain lessened. There is strength obtained from the suffering of the human spirit. Whenever we suffer, we cry to reach beyond the boundaries of the pain, and with every stretch beyond those boundaries, we grow stronger by the very act of reaching. Though I sorrowed for the suffering of mankind, my strength grew.

Nineteen sixty-four. Vietnam. I was thirteen and my father was going to war. I informed my parents that this was quite impossible, as Dad couldn't kill anyone. Regardless, I was told, he was a military man and he had his orders. It was his job. I wondered if it was just me, or if the world was really so insane. I could understand that one might be tempted to kill out of anger or hatred, but not because someone said it was their job. And now my father, who had instilled in me a respect for all nations, races and peoples, was being forced to view as an enemy a people he didn't even know. Our government claimed an enemy, but what did that have to do with him? How could a political structure have the control to wipe out a life at its whim? How could a man permit himself to be brainwashed into believing that the enemy created by a government was also his enemy? Have humans no mind of their own, or are they simply followers and victims of the establishment? I began to wonder if I were a victim — a wasted, miserable pawn in some cruel cosmic game. If I was, then like Shakespeare's Romeo I would "defy you stars!" I would not be a pawn, a victim or a follower for the amusement of anyone, earthly or otherwise.

My father was thirty-four when he went to Vietnam. The next year he returned home, changed, angry and sullen, but alive. He was one of the lucky ones.

Although I had no true friends, people liked to talk to me. It was a paradox. They confided in me their secrets and problems but never made an effort to associate with me beyond that. By then I had created such an energy of "I know you won't like me, so leave me alone," that only the most determined were willing to penetrate my cage to meet the person within. But they liked to share with me their hurts and joys — the pendulum swing of emotions typical of the teenager. Even though I had not experienced their lives, I knew what they were feeling. And I knew it from a point of strength, not of sorrow or becoming swallowed up in their pain. From a detached place, I understood, and with a strong calm, I listened. And listened. There was no judgment to be made, as I never saw anyone to be in the wrong. I merely saw them as having varying viewpoints. Since I rarely spoke to anyone, I never told this one what that one said. As keeping silent and holding a secret were two things at which I was excellent, I became the mother confessor for many of my peers — a position I resented at the time. To whom would I confess? Of course, even if there were someone available I wouldn't have trusted anyone enough to voice my feelings.

By the time I was fifteen, my feeling of not belonging and my constant withdrawal eventually sent me into a dangerous depression that lasted several months. It was summer vacation, and I slept twenty hours a day. I would go to bed around seven at night and sleep until late afternoon the next day. I had nightmares, didn't eat, didn't speak and didn't leave the house. My parents were beside themselves. They had never realized that their daughter's uncommunicative behavior was covering up severe emotional distress. I thought myself grand! I was surely the world's greatest actress for being able to hide (even from my parents!) the endless hurricane that raged within me. I had not intended to deceive them, but the fact that I had, stirred a perverse sense of accomplishment in me.

During this time my mother became pregnant. I saw it as a curse and a slap in my face. She implied to me that I was a disappointment as a daughter, and stated that whatever she had done wrong with me was not going to be repeated with the new family she had planned. From the time I was fifteen to nineteen years old, she gave birth to two boys and one girl. True to her word, she did not do to them as she had to me. They were loved. They were fussed over and coddled, but most importantly, they were "normal." I resented them to the core of my being.

Nineteen sixty-seven. Back to Germany. "Home." We lived in a village high in the mountains. I was considered German and treated as such by the people. The respectful and affectionate treatment I received from my German peers was a new experience to which I couldn't relate at all. Instead of being tall and homely, I was now considered to be statuesque and pretty. I marveled at how fickle people could be. Inside I was still the same, so what did the outside matter? Nevertheless, this new attention felt wonderful. The Germans honestly liked me, and I kept wondering why.

Though I enjoyed the village (as best I was able to enjoy anything at that time), life in the American school was hell as usual. The American gangs seemed to have it in for me. I was attacked several times and found myself in knife fights.

Not one person from the school befriended me. I saw myself as too tall, too German, too light, too dark, definitely too quiet and now, too angry. I stood out like a sore thumb. Not only did I look different, but I had created an air of indifference about me that was interpreted as haughtiness and pride. I let this facade do the talking for me. It was the sort of energy that bullies took as a challenge, even though the last thing I wanted was to confront anyone; I just wanted to be left alone. But when attacked, all that pent-up silence burst forth with a wildness and force that astonished and terrified me. I thought I might seriously hurt someone some day if pushed too far, so I took as much as I could and retreated even more.

School was simply unbearable. After coming down with the flu which left me bedridden for several weeks, I began failing classes. Math was always my worst subject. One particular day the teacher had demonstrated a problem on the board and then instructed me to go to the board to figure the next problem. I was lost. I couldn't follow her explanation, let alone figure one out myself in front of the class. After making several incorrect guesses, I admitted that I didn't know how to do it. She yelled at me that she had already explained this many times, and that I must be stupid. I looked at her, threw the chalk on the floor and walked out. I never again returned to that class. There were several such incidents. At that point I was too weary to care.

I had become quite powerful in the oddest ways, I thought. Even though I saw myself as pathetic, I was aware of appearing very strong to other people. I began to perceive a thick, brick wall extending six feet from my body and surrounding me. Those who met me, met the wall, and what this wall mirrored to them was usually quite distasteful. I wondered how long it had been there and whether I liked it or not. After all, it did protect me. I knew it presented an image of being hard, cold and impenetrable — not at all who I was. However, there was the occasional person who, using some inner soul quality, had the vision to penetrate my barricade. Such people were very rare, but all had the quality of gentleness and openness about them. I questioned how they could survive in such a hateful world, being so open. On one hand I envied them, but on the other was thankful for my wall.

I noticed that I had also become very bold, with a "Damn the torpedoes!" sort of attitude. I was fiercely loyal to myself and fearlessly took responsibility for my actions, be they right or wrong, sanctioned or reproached. This attitude was very trying for my parents. Not that I ever got in any real trouble, but if I honestly felt I was in the right, I would point-blank defy them. I would do what I wanted most, and that was to get away from Americans and school!

So, rather than exit the bus at the school after the forty-five minute ride down the mountain, I would get off in the city and hang out, catching the bus back up the mountain at the end of the day. I spent a considerable amount of time in the German clubs that were open twenty-four hours. I walked a lot and on two separate occasions helped two girls run away from home. I found them each shelter, kept them fed, and as usual, told no one. Both girls had abusive, tyrannical mothers and were perfect candidates for living on the streets. Not that running away was really the answer, of course, but at the time it seemed the only available choice. When one of the girls was finally found by the police, my name was mentioned. She ran away again, and that time her parents came after me with both barrels loaded! At two a.m. one morning we were awakened by a very hysterical woman and her hen-pecked husband. Calling me every name she could, she demanded to know if I had aided and encouraged her daughter to run away, and had I, myself, not attended school for a month? With my parents in bewildered astonishment, I answered "yes" and "yes." She would have the military police after me! She would have me arrested! She would guarantee my immediate deportation! My father informed her husband that he had better remove this woman from our house or he would do the honors himself. They left. Next came the parent/daughter showdown.

I was frequenting bars? How was I managing this, not being eighteen yet? I hadn't been to school for a month? Not only that, but I had been hitch-hiking down the mountain in the middle of the night and hitch-hiking back in time to get dressed and go the school? They honestly didn't understand, and because they didn't understand, my heart hurt for them and for me. I especially hurt for my father. Though we never had a close relationship, I always thought he was a wonderful human being. He was tall and strong, always honest, and acted with high morals and ethics. He was reserved with a quiet strength of character that I admired. But now I had hurt him. The realization that he had failed to take action regarding my emotional problems hit him like a ton of bricks. He felt like a failure. I had let him down, and I was devastated.

After this incident I sank into a deep depression from which there seemed to be no way out.

The mind is a fascinating thing. Even then I spent hours thinking, analyzing and wondering why people acted the way they did. I examined my feelings, and then I examined theirs. I realized that my capacity for listening and understanding without judgment led me into a marvelous world unknown to most; a world of horrors, joys and twisted tunnels leading into the unknown — the incredible world of the mind.

But I also saw it as fragile, and as I watched the muddied tidal wave of emotions sweep dangerously close to my hovel of sanity, I began to fear the possibility of losing my mind. This thought forced me to recognize my need to express myself, but someone had to help me. My parents seemed to have the same idea, because shortly after the ordeal with the raving mother, my father asked me if I would like to see a psychiatrist. I was thrilled! For fifty minutes once a week, someone would listen to me. I would force myself to communicate and if I were lucky, he might even understand me.

I began therapy with the good doctor — a Freudian child psychiatrist. Within one semester my grades went from "F" to "C." I started to feel there was some hope for my future. Perhaps I would find peace, maybe even become "normal." I luxuriated in the German countryside and felt myself beginning to heal. For hours I would walk in the forest or sit in the ranger's look-out tower in search of elk and wild boar. I sat in the farmer's grain fields, hidden by the grain which towered over my head. I felt at peace with the trees, the farmer's fields, the clean air and the simple life of these gentle village people. I was almost eighteen, and decided I would remain in Germany after my parents went back to the States. In Germany I would heal. I would finally have a home.

At the time I had dual citizenship — German by birth and American by adoption. At eighteen I would legally lose one of those citizenships. The one I would retain was determined by the country in which I lived. Germany had recently lost the war to Americans, and my mother, even though German herself, never wanted me to become a German citizen. With Germany's history of war she feared that if I remained, I might also experience such devastation within my lifetime. I wanted to stay in Germany. She made it clear that I was returning to the States before I was eighteen. As I had made up my school credits and would be graduating within a year, I begged my parents to let me remain in Germany and live in the American dormitory. I needed the clean air, high mountains and pine trees to heal me, whereas the flat lowland and desert of southern California seemed to scar or harm me in some way. Nevertheless, I was forced to return to the U.S., kicking and screaming the whole way.

I returned to the States in the middle of my junior year. Serendipitously, after having been in school only two weeks, I met a boy who became my best friend — the best friend I had never had. I was as happy as I was capable of being. The month I graduated from high school we moved in together. Within a year we were married, and remained so for the next five. He and I were crazy about each other. He understood me on the deepest levels. For the first time in my life I really opened up and communicated. I had learned to talk with the psychiatrist, but I never really had learned to communicate. He thought I was gorgeous, intelligent, talented, stimulating and not only did he love me, but he also liked me. What concepts! I had never thought of myself in any of those terms. We went to college full-time and worked part-time. We both majored in psychology (what else?) and minored in sociology.

Throughout our relationship I was constantly trying to pull myself back together emotionally, and wearied of what seemed like an endless battle. My husband could always go a little bit further than me — always a step ahead. We studied for exams. He made "A's" while I made "C's." He went through graduate school on grants and scholarships; I dropped out. I was well-read, but he was a walking library. I wrote poetry, but his poetry was published. I never resented him for this nor was I ever in competition with him, yet he was a constant reminder of what I perceived to be my inadequacies. In my own mind, I could never make the grade.

One of the things that he said he loved about me was that I was "different." The very "different" that had tormented me all my life. Not to think of being different as bad, but merely … different, was a new perspective he had given me. He felt my insight and understanding into people was extraordinary. Because I was a fiercely loyal and honest person who didn't play the social or relationship games, people didn't quite know how to categorize me. There weren't any pigeon holes into which I fit. I also had a strength of character that surpassed most. These were what he considered to be my major attributes. His favorite phrase to me was, "Don't let the bastards get you down." The "bastards" were everyone who maligned me, criticized me unfairly, or treated me in any way without due respect. In my mind, that covered just about everyone.

I held on to that phrase for many years as it gave me a new perspective of myself. It had a sense of fighting back which made me feel empowered. As much as I really appreciated his view of me and his support, my feelings of insecurity and lack of worthiness overshadowed any positive qualities he saw. All I knew was that I was different and that I didn't belong. I hoped that through my marriage to him my sense of belonging might grow.

It was during the period we were together that I had my first metaphysical experience. At that time, I had absolutely no understanding of the other realms, metaphysics, or energy. I did, however, have some concept of the Christian heaven and hell, angels and demons, though I wasn't sure I believed in any of it. I certainly had no psychic abilities of which I was aware. My husband was working out of town three days a week. During the nights he was gone, I began to have what I considered to be an irrational fear of something evil in my bedroom. So much so, that I found myself hiding under the covers at night, clutching a Bible. I felt that my fears and behavior were totally irrational, but there was no mistaking that feeling of evil. Where it came from I didn't know, but it hovered over me at night, evoking terror in my heart.

One evening I was sitting in my living room facing my bedroom. To my amazement I suddenly saw the figure of a man, suspended approximately two feet above the floor in my bedroom doorway. He was totally invisible, yet I could see him perfectly. He wore a black robe and had a heinous countenance as he stared directly at me. Then it seemed that he attained some control over my body, and I began to jerk and tremble uncontrollably. A fearful thought of the Christian tales of demonic possession entered my mind. As I said, this was my first taste of the supernatural, and I didn't like it at all. My hope was that if there were this dark side, maybe there was a light side as well. If not, I was really in trouble! I heard myself calling for God to help me.

For some reason, at that point I looked to my left. There, standing about two feet off of the ground, was another transparent male figure, this one wearing a white robe. He was staring at the "demon." I then looked to the right and saw yet another "angelic being," exactly like the one to the left, but this one looked down at me and smiled! It was a smile of such love, comfort and strength such as I'd never experienced in this life. I was thrilled! A real angel had smiled at me! When I looked back at the dark being, he was gone. I looked to my left and right, and the light beings were also gone. The tremors and jerking stopped as I regained control of my body.

After that experience, the evil energy never again returned to my bedroom. All things considered, I felt quite wonderful, but totally baffled. What was that all about, and why me? It was not until many years later that I was to understand the purpose of this event — it was a foresight into the work I would do later and the beings who would be assisting me.

A year after this incident, my husband applied for graduate school. University of Kentucky, Lexington and UCLA offered him the most in scholarship and grant money. As prestigious as UCLA would have appeared on his resume, I simply had to get out of the smog and heat. I wanted out of California, and if he were accepted in Kentucky, I wanted to go there. All I knew about Kentucky was that it had horses, bluegrass, rolling hills and was neutral in the Civil War. That was enough for me! When we were twenty-five, we loaded the top of our VW bug, put the dog and cat in the back seat and drove two-thousand miles to the Bluegrass State.

Up to this time, my idea of life was totally unrealistic. Put simply, I hadn't a clue. My husband was the only friend I had had, and he and I were going to do this "life" thing together. I wasn't concerned that I had dropped out of school, because he was going to finish his Masters, make lots of money and we would live happily ever after. It was a simple, certain plan on which we both agreed. A support to this plan was my strong belief in friendship. Never having had a friend, when I got one I was loyal to the core. "Lovers come and go, but friends are forever," was my belief.

When we arrived in Kentucky, the grant money and a part-time job was waiting for him. He began work immediately, generally arriving home around seven p.m.. We had been in Kentucky only a month when he failed to come home one night, arriving instead at six the next morning. His explanation and my response were simple, to the point and painfully honest, as it should be among friends.

"Where have you been?"

His answer was matter-of-fact and well planned. He had gotten married too young and had never really had a chance to kick up his heels. He felt himself to be too much a part of me and wanted his own identity. He had found a girlfriend, had slept with her that night and intended to keep her. He expressed his sorrow for hurting me, but felt that he couldn't deny himself what he needed to do. The rest was up to me.

With amazing non-judgmental calm, I listened. I understood. He had to do what he had to do. He had betrayed my trust, and I didn't want that reminder around me, so divorce was the only answer. We would find an attorney the next day. Two months later we were divorced. It was a very "nice" divorce. We went to the attorney together to file the petition. We divided our belongings with dignity. We were very concerned for each other's welfare.

The day of the divorce he was to pick me up and we were to go to court together. That morning, however, he called me crying, saying that I was the best friend he had ever had and he couldn't bear to be there to finalize the separation. Would I mind going without him? Of course not. I went through the chilling ordeal alone, came home, called him and said that we were now divorced. He tearfully apologized for not being there to support me at the courthouse. No problem. No problem at all. I wasn't going to let the bastard get me down.

To all appearances, I seemed to be very controlled throughout the two months prior to the divorce. That was not the case at all. Or perhaps it was; I didn't know. I didn't know what part of me was running the show. I was falling apart, and yet I was functioning. I was strong as an ox, yet I was whipped down. I had pulled up the personality, the actress that my parents had seen for eighteen years. It was the mask I put on for the world. Then, one afternoon alone in my apartment, I looked at myself in the bathroom mirror and to my horror, the mask cracked.

I watched in terror as my face transfigured into some ghoulish monster, and I felt my sanity leave me. I screamed at the sight and fell on the floor hysterically screaming and sobbing. I couldn't hold it together anymore! My mind! My mind! I was losing my mind!

"Get up!" A man's voice, loud and strong, boomed in my head.

"Get up!" It was forceful. It was demanding. There was no one with me yet this man's voice was taking control. I tried to pull myself up, but I hadn't the strength. "I can't," I sobbed.

"Get up! Get up NOW!" Like a cat I clawed the bathroom wall, dragging myself to my feet.

"Go outside to the hall!" Crying and laughing, hysterical, senseless and unthinking, I flung myself against the walls of my apartment until I reached the front door. I opened the door and stood swaying in the hall of the apartment building.

"Knock on your neighbor's door!" I knocked. I had only known this neighbor for two weeks. He was a very mature and decent man, and I was very glad he was home. He laid me on his couch, threatening to take me to the hospital if I didn't pull myself together. Imagine his dilemma! Before the evening was over I was calmly drinking tea and talking normally. It was such a relief to feel my mind anchor back into my body. Surely the voice had saved me just in time, for such an episode never occurred again.

Oddly, at the time I never seriously questioned who or what the voice was. Having no metaphysical understanding, I believed that if a voice were in my head, it could come from nowhere other than me. At the time, this was the only reasonable conclusion I could draw. That the voice was strongly male and didn't sound at all like mine was beyond me. Many years later, my beloved friend and brother, Ashtar, of the Ashtar Command, told me it was his voice that I had heard, and it was he who had saved me from a total nervous breakdown that frightful afternoon. For those of you who do not know them, the Ashtar Command is an intergalactic fleet of starships, angelic and Light beings who are assisting Earth through her ascension.

With my husband gone, income was now a major challenge for the first time in my life. Prior to moving to Kentucky I had worked part-time jobs in mental health. Between the two of us, we had never had money to spare, but we had always managed. Now I had myself, rent and a cat and dog to support. I thought asking for alimony would be a cop-out. If he could make a living for himself, so could I. Other than the years that I was married, I had always felt alone, but this was alone of a different sort — no parents, husband, or friends and living in a strange city. Fortunately I had kept the car, so I diligently began applying for jobs in mental health. No luck. Typing, receptionist … no luck. Waitress, house cleaning … no luck. "Damn! Why has the world always resisted me? (Don't let the bastards get you down.) I refuse to become a victim to it! This is war, world! I can do it! Whatever it is, I can do it!"

There was an ad in the paper for nurse's aides at one of the local hospitals. It included a free two-week training period. If passed, one was guaranteed a job at the hospital.

Hospitals. In my mind, they were the most hideous places in the world next to mortuaries. Hospitals scared me. The smell made me sick, and my nerves bristled at the thought of needles, doctors and nurses. My father had been in the hospital once for a week, and I didn't even visit him because I couldn't stand to go through the doors. In my mind, hospitals held a world of sickness and death. A world I'd always wanted to avoid. Hospital, huh? O.K. I can do it.

I took the training and began working the third shift. My body totally rebelled at the new sleeping hours. I never got used to it. I was also required to do teamwork, which meant I had to interact with people — something which I found just about impossible to do. I spent every second of my free time sitting alone in the stairway or hiding in the bathroom. Being thrust into the adult world of social interaction was quite a learning experience for me. Mildly put, I was appalled! These people gossiped. I had never really been around gossip before and found it disgusting. They chattered about the most trivial nonsense and obviously considered themselves quite important. This last one really bewildered me. What did they see about themselves that was so important? Certainly I could find nothing superior about them. Not surprisingly, I was considered the most inferior of all. Not only was I at the bottom of the hierarchy, being a subservient nurse's aid, but I was considered very much the snob. This was due to the "leave me alone" air that I still carried, and because I never joined in on their chats, and certainly never volunteered any information about myself. As usual, I was disliked and friendless. I became painfully bored and needed more intellectual stimulation.

Within two weeks, I had approached administration about on-the-job training programs. Was there anything other than nursing that I might be able to learn? There was. It was in the department called the Heart Station, working as a Heart Station Technician. This was the department that did the EKG's, stress tests and a new, exciting procedure called echocardiography, "Echo" for short, which utilized ultrasound to visualize and diagnose heart disorders. It took a good deal of training, but I would be the first to be offered the position, should there be an opening.

In the meantime, I transferred from night shift to day shift in the Coronary Care Unit. On day shift in the CCU, I finally got a sense of what hospital work was really like. The hospital buzzed with activity during the day. The pace was fast, and there was no time for idle talk and gossip. I liked my patients and they liked me. I cheered them up, made them laugh and encouraged them. Whether they were angry and belligerent, or whimpering and afraid, I treated them all the same way — with kindness. I observed that not all medical staff did the same. In fact, I was often shocked at the callousness with which some patients were treated. But as for me, I was feeling useful and enjoying it.

I worked in the CCU for one year, then transferred to the Heart Station where I learned echocardiography. I was one of the pioneers in the field of diagnostic ultrasound, of which echocardiography was a part. Ultrasound became my career and livelihood for the next seventeen years. Eventually I would completely remove myself from allopathic medicine, dedicating myself instead to full-time wholistic and spiritual healing. But that would not happen for several years.

About two years after my divorce, another occasion arose in which I found myself quite alone and very much fighting for my rights. In an effort to find answers to the continual confusion that I encountered in my life, I looked toward organized religion. As far as religious education went, I had none. I had gone to church three times in my life; twice to a Baptist church and once to a Catholic church. The Catholic church absolutely scared me! There seemed to be so much ceremony with which I was very uncomfortable. The priest was ominous and I found the constant kneeling/sitting to be ridiculous and confusing. The whole organized religion thing was a mystery to me. In college I had studied world religions and religious philosophy. The Eastern teaching made sense, but I couldn't agree with the wrathful God of Christianity. Yet, in spite of my skepticism, I was searching and became involved in a fundamentalist Christian religion. It was one of those faiths in which members were told (in the most explicit detail) what they could and could not do. Anyone breaking these rules was publicly disfellowshipped or excommunicated. If someone were disfellowshipped, the church members were strictly forbidden to associate with him, or that member would be brought before the elders of the church and reprimanded.

Nevertheless, I devoted myself to that religion, studied the Bible fervently and became a champion proselytizer (another rule). There were two main reasons why I took to this path. The first and most sound reason was to find answers to the dilemma of life. In studying the Bible, I thought I would be using my thinking and reasoning faculties to figure out life's puzzles. I soon realized that I was not permitted to think but was, instead, *told* what to think.

Another reason for joining was to feel "normal" and obtain some sense of belonging. I had a stereotyped view of the happy family going to church together. I thought that through some form of osmosis, I might pick up that happy family feeling. I tried very hard to be a "good" Christian, but I had constant battles with my conscience. Members of this faith believed they were the chosen ones and only by believing in Jesus and being one of their members, could a person receive salvation. They believed their church elders were selected by God, therefore, their say and council was divine and not to be disputed.

I never, from the very beginning, had believed in a chosen religion or people. If God created everyone, why would he allow the few Christians to be "saved" and permit everyone else to be destroyed? This was absurd. To believe that people of different religious beliefs, such as Mohandas Gandhi or Martin Luther King, Jr., who had sacrificed themselves for the love of mankind, were not worthy of "saving" was ludicrous. Also, I more than once thought myself more loving and understanding than some of their "divinely ordained" elders. But, I dared speak none of my thoughts out loud. The short time that I was a member of this organization were truly the years of my greatest self-deception. I lived and professed an absolute lie to the public, and more horrendously, to myself — all in an attempt to belong.

Ironically, the phrase "Wherever you are, that's where you're at," fit me perfectly. I had taken my feeling of worthlessness, my desire to be alone (though wanting to be liked and welcomed) and my cover-up appearance of haughtiness with me. Nothing changed. I made no friends; I still felt disliked.

But I gave it my best effort, and in so doing thought that if I married someone of "the faith" we might become accepted as a couple, since I apparently wasn't accepted on my own. And that's what I did. Just as this religion expressed the opposite of what I really believed, I married a man who could not have been a worse mate for me if I had intentionally looked for one. His ego and pride were the size of Texas, and his attitude toward me was that of a superior whom I was to honor and obey. He ruled over me with an iron hand, telling me when I could leave the house, and when I was to return. I could go nowhere without informing him where I was going. He also forbade me to work. Unlike my relationship with my first husband, we definitely were not friends. Unfortunately, I realized none of these aspects of his personality prior to marrying him. When I discovered them and knew I couldn't live with it, I went to the church elders stating that we were having problems and needed counseling (still trying to be a good Christian). I was told it was something we needed to work out ourselves. They offered us no help.

One evening, after being married almost a year, we were engaged in a horrendous argument in which he threatened to throw me out of the house. To his surprise, I grabbed some clothes and left on my own. The next day I rented an efficiency apartment. (Against his will I had returned to work at the hospital and fortunately could rely on my own income.) He reported my insubordinate behavior to the elders. I was called before them and asked to explain my actions. I explained my viewpoint, but was instructed to immediately return to my husband and ask his forgiveness for my disrespectful behavior. I refused. I was threatened with being disfellowshipped for being rebellious to the church. I still refused. ("Don't let the bastards get you down.")

A tremendous realization washed over me that night as I sat before the board of elders and was pronounced disfellowshipped from the organization (and thereby supposedly from God). I understood that this organization was wrong for me; that what I needed was to follow my own truth. In other words, I realized that I could give myself permission to disagree. How simple! How amazing that it had taken me this long to understand that I could feel and believe differently from others and that it was all right. I didn't have to agree with anyone else, nor did anyone have to agree with me. And all this time I had felt that there was something wrong with me because my way of thinking was so different from that of most people. From then on, I remained true to my conscience. I never again compromised myself nor did I ever again come under the sway of public opinion.

Leaving the church that fall evening, I was overcome with a very familiar feeling. Alone. Miserably alone … again. I had made no friends at the church and only had working relationships with the people at the hospital. But with the feeling of being alone came another equally strong feeling — a new one this time — freedom. I had never been free before. I had always been a slave to opinion, and now I knew for a fact that opinion didn't matter. I also knew that my first husband was right when he had told me that there wasn't anything wrong with me. What I considered to be faults were actually attributes. But still, I was only one person, and it seemed like the whole world constantly opposed me. How could so many people be wrong? "Cattle," I thought, "humans are unthinking followers like cattle being led to the slaughterhouse." I was slightly shocked at hearing my own thoughts. Why did I think of "humans" as if they were something separate from myself? Well, there were many things that I neither knew nor understood. Maybe in my lifetime, if I were lucky, I would figure out the answers. But for the moment, I stood in the church parking lot by my car, gazing at the stars. I was very sad but happy, alone but free. I was going to find out who this "different" person was. I knew I could do it. I could do anything!

My second husband and I had been together a total of two years before the divorce was final. He contested the whole way, constantly had me followed and even called my attorney, threatening to shoot him in the courtroom. When the divorce was actually finalized, he left me alone. I never saw him again.

At this point I was twenty-eight years old and eager to start my life of freedom. I had come to grips with the idea that I neither needed nor wanted a husband again. I didn't care what people thought of me, and carried an air that said as much. I lived by myself, having neither roommates nor live-in lovers. I continued to read profusely and patronized all the fine arts both in Lexington and Cincinnati, Ohio. I frequented all horse performances, of which Lexington had many. I loved the steeplechase, harness racing, dressage and track racing. Though I never bet at the race tracks, I would guess which horse would place by watching and "feeling" them before lining up. I was astonishingly accurate.

Freedom was wonderful. Alone was fine. But I was never truly happy. I felt driven — driven to fit in and be "normal." I had nothing to live for and life had absolutely no meaning for me. Everything around me felt shallow, yet inside myself lay a deep, mysterious empty well that needed to be filled. If I didn't fill it, there would be no reason to stay alive. Somehow I had to find what was missing. Fitting in — being normal — was the only possible answer I could think of; the one thing I knew I didn't have. So, like Camelot's King Arthur, I wondered, "What do the simple folk do?" So I did what I thought they did in the hopes of finding the answer.

I began ballroom dancing. First I was a student, was told that I was a "natural" and then became an instructor. For five years I professionally taught dance and became a ballroom exhibition competitor. I loved dance and the feel of the studio. I danced in the evening after a full day at the hospital, and most Saturdays. My mind stayed busy with choreographing dance routines and the endless practice of technique and steps. However, dance is not a solitary activity. As insecure as I was, I was forced to be social, gracious and charming. This was very difficult for me as I felt like a phony. I didn't know how to be social or make small-talk, so I had to fake it, which made me feel even more insecure.

On Sundays, when the studio was closed, I often sat in the empty ballroom and wondered if I would ever accomplish excellence in anything. Just as I had wanted to be a champion equestrian, I wanted to be a champion ballroom dancer. I knew I had the talent, drive and will to accomplish anything that I desired, but situations that I believed to be beyond my control seemed to thwart my attempts before I could attain my goals. True to this pattern, within five years the studio closed. I was left without a dance partner and without a ballroom. The opportunity to further my dance career never presented itself to me again.

Most of my peers who were my age had a home — husband, kids and house. The husband and kids were definitely unappealing to me, but I bought a house with three bedrooms. (One for me, one for my dog, one for my cat, and my birds lived in the living room.) The purpose of buying the house was to make me settle down. I had moved within Lexington, every year. Definitely not "normal" behavior. I hoped that if I invested enough money, I might stay put. I also felt very aggressive about my career and became quite the businesswoman.

After living in Kentucky for about eight years, I had topped-out my salary as the highest paid echocardiographer in Lexington. I had reached a financial dead end, had owned my house for three years and was ready to sell it, and was past ready to move out of the state. I applied for various echocardiography jobs around the country and was accepted in Florida. Florida was a place I had visited twice, but really knew little about other than that it was hot, humid, had the most gigantic, aggressive flying cockroaches I had ever seen, and should have named the lizard the state animal. It really was not where I wanted to live.

Nevertheless, I felt I had overstayed my welcome in Kentucky, and it was time to move on. So, at thirty-three I packed up my animals, said good-bye to the Bluegrass State and headed for flat, muggy central Florida.

Although I didn't know it at the time, numerologically I was in a number nine year — the year of ending a nine-year cycle, resting and preparing to begin a new one.

And that's what I did... .

AWAKENING

Wake, oh Wake!
Run to the feet of your Beloved for
your Lord stands near to your head.
You have slept for unnumbered ages;
This morning will you not wake?

— Kabir, *Songs of Kabir*

When I was about twenty-nine, a haunting situation had occurred that I was never able to put out of my mind. In Florida the meaning to this situation became clear. I woke up one morning with a frightening "knowing." I knew that I wasn't human!

This knowledge touched all the way to the deepest level of my soul, completely filling me with fear and hopelessness. At that time, people were still questioning if extraterrestrials were real, and if there really could be life on other planets. I had no real opinions on the matter, but even if extraterrestrials did exist, they had nothing to do with me, or so I thought. But now, in my perpetual state of confusion, to wake up knowing that I wasn't human and that I didn't belong on this Earth, was just too much! I considered it another slap in the face from the Universe. Another, "See what a miserable wretch you are! You don't even belong on this planet." I was distraught! If I wasn't human, what was I, and if I didn't belong on Earth where did I come from — hatched from the sky? And what was I to do about it? Remain lost in a strange land for the rest of my life? Better to end the life, I thought. I even made a few feeble attempts at it but had too much of a fighting spirit to follow through completely.

In the meantime, I had cultivated a relationship with a particular woman at work and reluctantly told her about my discovery. As kindly as she could, knowing that I was quite serious, she said that I was really exceptionally sensitive, and it was this that made me so "special"; that I possessed qualities of the heart, insight and wisdom that far surpassed anyone she had ever met. What was wrong with that? She thought I just felt non-human because I had a "specialness" superior to most. Great! I didn't want to be special. I wanted to be like everyone else. Nonetheless, I never spoke of my secret identity again until several years had passed, and I was well-settled in Florida.

In Florida I became even more aggressive in my career. This was part of my usual search for the answer to what made the average person tick. Making money and acquiring "stuff" was my last attempt, and as far as I could see, my only hope for finding my niche among mainstream society. But, I continued to move every year or two, always restless, always looking for the elusive "something."

I had become self-employed and found that I did very well as a businesswoman. To all outward appearances I was professional, in control, very dependable and reliable — definitely a person you would want on your team. Professionally, I was well in demand. My social life also greatly improved as I had acquired such a business-like air, which provided a facade to hide all my feelings of self-doubt. I say "facade" for, as I had done most of my life, I was playing a role. Again, I had everyone fooled into believing that I was content as a successful businesswoman, when in truth I could have cared less about the business or the money. Though I was not happy in business, I found myself stuck. How could I get out and what was I to do? I needed something to live for; making money seemed like my last hope. After living in Florida for a few years, the answer came.

One day I was doing an ultrasound exam on a patient who was wearing several pieces of crystal jewelry. I had seen crystals hanging from people's rear-view mirrors in their cars, and I'd noticed them being worn as necklaces. I assumed it was a craze, but maybe they knew something that I didn't, so I asked my patient if there were some significance to crystals. She briefly explained that rocks have consciousness and can be used in healing. I thought she and her crystals were fairly strange. My sort of person! She suggested a metaphysical bookstore if I wanted more information.

I had never heard of metaphysics but was willing to find out what it was, so I went. The place awed me! There was so much neat stuff everywhere I felt like I was in a grown-up toy store. And books — about all kinds of things that I had never heard of. I was in heaven! The owner was there that day and explained how to use a crystal pendulum. She handed me one and suggested that I try it. I asked its answer for "yes" and it swung one way, and for "no" it swung another way. Well, I was flabbergasted! Since I was looking for the perfect stone for myself, she suggested I pick out stones I was drawn to, then ask the pendulum, one by one, if this was the perfect stone for me. I lined up my stones, but was told "no" for each one. My enthusiasm was beginning to wane. Why couldn't I find a stone? The owner then suggested I ask if there was a stone in the entire store that was just right for me. Again I got a "no." Well, it was just too much! I was so weird that even a rock didn't want me! I became markedly upset. Upon seeing this, the owner sought to reassure me by saying that it would be difficult to find a stone that would resonate perfectly with me, as my aura showed that I was clearly not from this planet!

I must have had the most idiotic, dumbfounded look on my face when she said that. Could she really be confirming what I knew about myself? Then she suggested a book on incarnate extraterrestrials, which I bought and finished by dawn the next day. I recognized myself in the book, though I hadn't yet put it all together and I certainly didn't know what it all meant. However, I did know that somewhere, there were the answers about myself that I had been looking for. I was going to find those answers!

A week later I attended a workshop at the bookstore. I was lying on a mat doing a visualization exercise, when an energy overtook my body that was so intense and powerful that I felt myself lift off the floor. Then, for the second time in my life, I heard a powerful male voice boom a command in my head, "Wake up! The time is now! Wake up! The time is now!" I was astounded! Wake up from what? Wake up from my unconscious sleep, I thought. Wake up to the truth! I was going to find the truth. Finally!

From here the focus of my life completely changed. Now that a door had been opened, I lunged through. Absolutely nothing and nobody was going to stop me from finding out who I was and why I was here. I still worked to support myself, of course, but my interest in my career greatly waned. In fact, it eventually became a burden as it took up too much of the time I wanted to dedicate to studying, self-healing and meditation. But for the time being, the job was necessary.

I began my awakening by associating with metaphysical people, meditating, and of course reading, reading and reading. There was no end to my studying of spiritual practices and truths. I devoured the works of Paramahansa Yogananda and became a Kriya initiate, though not through his organization. I studied the Eastern Masters, Madam Blavatsky and Theosophy, the Master Djwhal Khul through Alice Bailey, Edgar Cayce through the A.R.E., and on and on. I also delved into a countless number of healing modalities, learning the spiritual make-up of the human energy systems, how they interrelated, the root cause of disease and different means to heal that cause.

In my desire to open up spiritually, I intuitively knew to meditate. Guided visualization meditation was not satisfactory for me, probably because I didn't feel really challenged and became somewhat bored. I wanted to find out what was inside of *me*. I wanted to meet the inner me. So somehow, instinctively, I found myself meditating "into the silence." What a wonderful place in which to be! In that space, understanding would flood my conscious mind. The puzzle pieces of my life began to come together, and behind the chaos I sensed order — teasing and coaxing me onward in my search.

Shortly after I had begun meditating, I was curling up for sleep one night and, once again, heard a voice in my head. This voice was different from the other two occasions — much softer, but still male. "I have something to tell you," he said. He then proceeded to give me some direction regarding my spiritual growth. For the spiritual neophyte that I considered myself to be, this was quite a phenomenon! As this voice was conversational, unlike the other two occasions, I felt a desire to communicate with it. "Who and what is talking in my head?" I asked. "Are you an angel, a dead person or an E.T.?" He replied, with gentle humor, "If I told you what I was you'd be confused, and you're confused enough already!" Thus began my relationship with Andronymous (know as Andromeda to some). Andronymous is a co-worker with Ashtar on the intergalactic fleet of starships, the Ashtar Command.

Between my guidance from Andronymous, my strong desire for spiritual awakening and my meditations, my spiritual growth expanded by leaps and bounds. I was directed to strengthen my aura and expand the abilities of my mind. To do so I began healing my bodies on all levels, and during my meditations I practiced different techniques to achieve mental clarity and control.

And so I grew, but it was a far from easy process. As usual, I was presented with obstacle after obstacle. The man I had been dating held the opinion that metaphysics was a very dangerous thing. "New Age" it was called, and these New Age people claimed they were God. How blasphemous! He also told me (and I had heard it from other sources as well) that when dealing in metaphysics and the other realms, there was great danger as dark spirits lived in those realms who could easily influence or even control one.

I had some knowledge of dark spirits from my encounter in California, and I really wanted nothing more to do with them. But it seemed that the answer to my self-identity questions and my intergalactic origins lay somewhere within this New Age thing. To discover who I was would entail taking a giant step into the unknown, possibly even resulting in harm to myself. I honestly considered all this. The dark realms were scary. How well I remembered that horrible dark being that controlled my body that afternoon in California, and how frightened I was at the evil that had surrounded me every night for the two previous weeks. But had not two angelic beings rescued me? Had not one smiled at me with such overwhelming love? Surely they would rescue me again, if need be. Should I deny myself the knowledge of my Self for fear of the unknown? No. I had finally found something to live for; and if necessary, paradoxically, I would die to obtain it.

My boyfriend temporarily left the state for Ohio. One night he called to tell me that he'd prayed that I be protected from the evil I was getting myself into. He said that after his petition for me, he felt a tremendous heat and energy come over him, making him feel as strong as Hercules. During a snowstorm in the middle of the night, he went outside stark naked and sat in the snow, "absorbing power." I had no idea what this meant, but it didn't sound good. After that night and for the next two months, he would call and tell me what I was wearing, where I was in the house, who I had been with and what we had done. How did he suddenly know these things, I asked. He replied that since he had given himself to "God" this "power" had been given to him to watch over me, supposedly to protect me from New Age harm. I was getting pretty scared by this time. None of this made any sense to me. What's more, whenever he phoned, a chilling feeling of evil would surround me, as if it slithered through the telephone wire. I didn't understand how these things worked, but I felt that something evil had happened to him and that we needed to break all ties. When I mentioned this he became enraged but then confessed the *entire* story of what he had done.

The night that he had prayed for me, he had actually asked "someone out there" to give him power over me. Two dark etheric beings appeared before him. He said they were almost totally physical, he could see them so clearly. He was told that he would receive superhuman powers and abilities with which to protect me, but in so doing, he would lose me in the end. He agreed. What they didn't tell him was that they would also torment him. From that time onward he spent hours each night witness to gruesome visions of the future — wars, plagues, mass murders — all of which he believed, and the sight of which tortured him. When he realized that the nightly visions might never end, he asked to renege on his agreement. He was told absolutely not, and the exhausting visions became even more frequent. In anguish he realized what he had done and sought to end his life, but then he began seeing visions of his afterlife in which he was tortured in a ghoulish hell. All this he told me as I was attempting to end our relationship. And so, as further fulfillment of his fiendish pact, he was losing me.

I was horrified beyond belief! He had made a literal pact with the devil. I didn't know such things could really happen other than in books or horror stories — Hollywood maybe, but not in real life. I emphatically stated I never wanted to see or hear from him again. He was livid and threatened my life. I was terribly afraid, but thank goodness he was a thousand miles away. Yet, he had attained such abilities, what might he be able to do transcending time and space? How odd that he was the one resistant to the other realms, yet in his fervor, became engulfed by it. The last day that I spoke to him, when the truth was finally revealed, was Christmas day, the celebrated day of the Christ's birth. How strange it all was!

I never saw or heard from him again, but my fear did not end there. It seemed there was much I needed to learn and the Universe was going to make sure that I learned it — and that I learned it well. The lesson dealt with this whole realm of Dark Forces, otherwise known as devils or demons. Of course, in retrospect, I see that the experience was to prepare me for the spiritual work that I was to do. Little did I know that, along with other forms of interdimensional work, I would be rescuing and releasing these dark beings.

Though my ex-boyfriend never called me again, the dark beings remained in my house. They would manifest in the patterns on my rug, on the walls of my house, hover around me at night and physically attack me as I slept. The latter was horrendous! I would wake up screaming, fighting them off. Through all this horror, I was aware of my spiritual guidance observing me. They reminded me that the Dark Forces never "got" to me. Other than scaring me half to death, they never hurt me or penetrated my auric field, and they always went away when I called for help.

There was something for me to learn here. Not only was I invulnerable to these Dark Forces, but fear was a useless waste of energy. This was a lesson that did not come easily, nor did I grasp it overnight. I later learned that not everyone is invulnerable to the dark beings. They can, indeed, penetrate and harm people, and frequently do. But in my case, I was being well protected so that I could experience them from a place of safety. From this emotionally harrowing, yet slightly detached place, I became an observer of these beings, learning their tricks, their weaknesses and their beliefs. Concurrently I learned how to rescue them from their own illusions and help them release their grip upon their victims.

At some point, I became aware of the existence of earthbound discarnates and their ability to attach to people's energy fields. I found this concept to be grim but intriguing, and was curious about the consciousness of such attachments. What did they think? Or did they?

During this time I had a friend who professed to have some knowledge of these beings. He was a healer who could project very strong healing energies through his hands, claiming the energy was so strong that Dark Forces and discarnates would jump out of his client's body. On one hand, this made sense to me, but on the other I thought, "So they jump out of the body and go where? Stand in the corner waiting, and then reenter their host when they're ready to go home?"

Understand, at this point I was very young in my "awakening" and people with any type of healing or spiritual abilities left me in awe. This healer friend of mine had hands that turned as hot as embers when he worked. Mine barely got warm on a good day. That I could "cast out" entities would be a miracle to me, yet I was so curious and wanted so badly to understand them that I thought I would give this entity-releasement thing a try.

I had a willing volunteer for my first releasement experiment. My plan was to project energy, in the form of Light, through my hands (I had my doubts, here) and into her crown. I would then speak generally to all my volunteer's attachments and ask them to enter the Light. Between the two of us, I hoped one would know if anything were happening.

We closed our eyes and proceeded. With utter amazement, in my mind's eye I saw thousands of cute, short E.T.'s making a long line to the pillar of Light. Inside the pillar was a spaceship that they entered. I decided that my imagination had just gone too far with this one! I asked my friend if she perceived anything. She said "Yes." She saw thousands of little E.T.'s going into a spaceship and into the Light. The last extraterrestrial was a little girl who waved to us, said "Bye!" and zipped up the Light into the ship. Then we saw the ship leave. We were astounded! What in the world was that all about? I continued to hold the Light to her head, sensing there was more — and there was. Her ex-mother-in-law appeared. They carried on a conversation and then the mother-in-law entered the pillar of Light. Then a couple of other people also appeared and were directed to the Light.

This was a profound experience for the neophyte I considered myself to be. I realized that discarnates could be communicated with and would communicate back. They were lost and confused, and with some patience and understanding, they could be relieved of their anxiety and directed to further their spiritual growth. It was a kinder, gentler method of entity-releasement than my healer friend used, whose emphasis was to remove entities from the host, never giving the entity itself a second thought. Remember, this took place at a time when very few people had any concept of attachments. Exorcism was considered to be a scary, horrendous thing practiced by the Catholic Church, and anything needing to be exorcised was thought dark and evil, and certainly not worthy of any kindness. There were, at the time, people who spoke to the dead, but removing the dead from one's energy field was another story. In fact, many times a clairvoyant would see an entity in someone's aura and profess it to be his or her spirit guide, when it was actually a parasitic discarnate. So for the most part, when it came to attachments, discarnates and Dark Forces, we were, if you'll excuse the pun, in the dark.

I also learned from my trial releasement that I could project Light. At the time, I didn't know if there was "Light" actually coming through my hands or not, but where I doubted my abilities with my hands, I knew for a fact that I had created Light with my mind. And finally, I also realized that even though I didn't see the little E.T.'s in brilliant color, I did, nonetheless, see them. Confirmed by my friend, I had had my first experience of clairvoyant inner vision.

At the time, none of us had any idea how common entity attachments were. I wanted to know if I had any myself, and if I did I wanted them gone. I tried tuning into myself, creating a pillar of Light and asking whoever was in there to leave. I had little confidence in myself with this technique. Sometimes I felt successful. Sometimes I didn't. If I "saw" something, I thought I was making it up. It was at this time that I met a 70+ year-old clairvoyant and psychic who became my dear friend. I asked her if she saw any discarnate attachments in my energy field and she said that she did. Could and would she remove them? She said "Yes" to both.

The process entailed placing her hands on my head, invoking the Light and asking the angels and Masters to take these beings from me. Within seconds she confirmed that they had all left. This was a new concept for me — asking the angels and Masters to take the entities to the Light. I stored it in the back of my mind. Still I wondered what these entities thought and felt, especially after we just kicked them out of their nice, comfy home in my body? And how did I know if they had all gone into the Light? What if some had just detached from my body and avoided the Light, or what if some simply refused to leave? Could they come back?

This, however, was not the end of my attachments. The next day I felt "heavy" and returned to my friend to see if I was reattached. I was. She said that my attachments were coming at night while I slept and that my house was full of them. What a situation! How in the world was I to protect myself when I slept? I had continuously worked on strengthening my aura and mind. I meditated and was totally dedicated to my spiritual growth, but this entity and Dark Force business was really getting to me! And why did no one else have these problems? Maybe they did and simply weren't aware of them. Whatever the case, I felt more than a little frustrated and alone.

My friend did another releasement on me. During the process, a being instructed her to tell me that I would never become attached again. It sounded good, but I hardly believed it. How could I be so lucky, and why would I no longer be attached? What was the difference between that day and the day before?

With moderate hopes, I retired to bed that night. Sometime during the night I was awakened by an incredibly evil energy in my bedroom, and by "things" beating against my aura. It was as if my aura were made of thick glass and they were throwing themselves against it, attempting to break through. My terror was beyond words! I prayed. I invoked every Light being I could think of. I repeated mantras over and over. This lasted for two hours, until eventually, out of total exhaustion, I fell back to sleep.

The next morning I hurried to my friend's house, totally upset and in a panic. I was attacked during the night! There must have been hundreds of them! I had fought them off for as long as I could, but surely they had all entered me when I had fallen asleep. I was undoubtedly the most possessed person in town, by now! She looked at me and calmly stated that I did not have a single discarnate attachment. Had I not been promised such? Where was my trust?

I have never had an entity attach itself to my energy field since.

I observed that my aura had become impenetrable "overnight." The timing, of course, was no accident as there are no accidents when we go through our growth experiences. Prior to this night, these entities were able to come and go through my aura at will, and I was not able to feel it, as their energy would mingle with mine. Since then, whenever anything of a low vibration comes in contact with me, I feel it immediately as it hits the barrier of my aura.

About a year after the incident with the entities, my guidance directed me to take a house in a small, rural town by the ocean. The house was two years old, on a dead-end dirt road which backed into woods. The town had a gas station, police station, post office and junk store, but no grocery store. There was something about this town that I really didn't like. A creepy feeling would come over me as I drove into it, and when I pulled onto my road I would feel the energy of something sinister. Aside from this energy, which in the beginning I ignored (I never ignore this sort of thing now!), the house and location among the trees, away from the big city, were ideal … or so I thought.

I was going to share this house with my clairvoyant friend who had moved in a week before me. When I moved in, bags in hand, cat, dog and birds in tow, the news she greeted me with was grim. At night, as she sat in the living room with the house locked, someone would turn the door handle trying to open the door. When she looked out the window, no one was there. She heard someone scratching on her bedroom window at night, but could find no one there either. In the morning she would see a man's footprints in the dirt of the flower bed along the outside wall. I asked my guidance, "Was this just a sick joke that I was directed to move here? How about I go back where I came from?" No such luck. I was to live there. And if that weren't bad enough, the house was haunted! And not just with your simple, confused dead person. It couldn't be so easy! We had vicious poltergeists who kept us up all night, creating the most ungodly noises from the walls and ceiling, flicking lights on and off, swinging our chandelier, and filling the house with a most threatening air.

In the interim we began to receive anonymous, threatening phone calls. My friend became ill and within two months her cat developed bone cancer and died. I was afraid for us and for my animals, but still my guidance said I had been directed to live there for a while, so I stayed.

We would frequently bring plants into the house in hopes of clearing the air, but they never lived. If we placed a healthy plant on our living room coffee table in the morning, by evening it would be totally wilted. We felt that there might be something in the ground under the house inundating us with these terrible energies, so one evening we decided to find out. My friend projected herself into the land under the house where she found the most horrible sight — a pit in which people had been buried alive. Not too long ago, this rural town had been the roaming grounds for certain Native American tribes. The Indians would capture the Spaniards as they sailed down the river, then torture and bury them alive in this huge pit. Of all things, our house was built right over this pit. The whole town was full of astral plane warring and slaughtering, still going on to that day. My friend and I called in all of our spiritual guidance and a huge Light. We directed and saw thousands upon thousands of souls entering this Light. The next day we did it again. We continued to release souls under the ground, in the woods, in the house, and throughout the town. It seemed endless. The energy improved by about fifty percent, but it was still far from comfortable. After six months, I was finally told that I could leave. Neither my animals nor myself had been harmed or attached.

As usual, there was a growth experience and lesson for me in all of this. I had been of great service to the astral plane, releasing huge numbers of discarnate souls. The ever-present "fear is futile" lesson was there, and I also felt that I had undergone a minor spiritual initiation. I believe that when we can endure horrendous situations without losing our spiritual faith or integrity, we have accomplished far more than we may realize on the physical plane. The Universe coaxes us on through any number of painful or fearful situations, and after we have endured, it rewards us, each reward being a confirmation of our spiritual growth. My first such reward occurred when I was told that I would no longer become reattached by discarnate beings. By remaining in this small town and keeping my integrity through it all, I was again rewarded by finding a perfect, airy, well-lit house with a large yard and trees, in an ideal neighborhood in another town. It was a wonderful relief!

By this time, my Dark Force and discarnate harassment had ended and I had become very proficient at feeling and clearing energies and discarnates in general, though I had not yet attained a proficiency at clearing discarnates specifically from people's energy fields; that was to come later. I gave my new house a thorough energy cleaning, found a couple of dead people, sent them on, and settled into a relative heaven.

In my wholistic wanderings, I decided to look into hypnosis. One of my acquaintances had a practice doing hypnosis, past-life regression and entity-releasement. I was fascinated with the thought of doing entity-releasement in a private practice. He offered courses in all of the above, which I took, certifying me as a hypnotherapist by the American Board of Hypnotherapy and the National Guild of Hypnotists.

The entity-releasement technique was wonderful and very close to what I was looking for. The client, or host, is put into an altered state. The therapist then asks certain questions which draw an entity to speak. This dialogue is carried on through the client, who feels as if the entity's thoughts are her own. The therapist converses with and educates the discarnate, and then directs him to look for the Light, which appears when the discarnate draws his attention to it.

There were a few flaws with this technique. The host usually could only access one entity at a time. Sometimes that would take up to one and one-half hours, or an entire session. Sometimes the host did not have the ability to access her attachments, and sometimes the entity "hid" and refused to talk. Even so, it was a good start and certainly an improvement over what anyone else I knew was doing.

I began doing releasement work on anyone who would let me. This scared a lot of people who preferred to stay in ignorance as to who or what was time-sharing their body. But the brave ones came. I had many, many conversations with many, many dead people. Their stories and situations are fascinating, to be sure. One can be certain that rescuing these beings is a tremendous service to the astral plane — certainly no less important or helpful than assisting people who are still abiding in their physical bodies.

There was one more aspect of this technique I was still to learn. When talking to a discarnate, sometimes it turns out not to be a discarnate, but a Dark Force. Then what was I to do? I was directed to Dr. Bill Baldwin and his wife Judith. Bill was the leading pioneer in Dark Force research and was coming to town to give a workshop. Of course I attended!

Through his inner guidance, Bill discovered a technique, using the Archangel Michael and his band of angels, to talk to the Dark Force through the client. Michael holds the Dark Force bound, while Bill uses some wonderful techniques to reason with the Force. Following this, the Dark Force, by his own choice, walks away from the dark and is escorted to the Light by Michael's angels. Bill and Judith work as a team. He talks to the dark one through the client as is done with discarnate release, while Judith clairvoyantly sees the dark attachments so they cannot hide from Bill.

One thing Bill said in his class that astounded me was that everyone had Dark Forces, unless they had been released. My clairvoyant friend had long ago released all my discarnates, and I had never been reattached, but Dark Forces were a different matter. I learned that they attach early in life and remain with us. Well, that included me! I was horrified at the thought of sharing my body with those dreadful things. After all, I had had enough encounters with them over the years and knew how threatening they could be. To think that they could be a part of me was horrendous!

As the universe would have it (just to make sure that I didn't get away with anything, no doubt) I was one of those picked to be exorcised in front of the class. It was absolutely dreadful! The most evil, vicious, foul-mouthed, aggressive Dark Force exploded from me and took out his wrath on Bill. As I was speaking the dark one's thoughts, a part of me wondered how this could even be possible. How could something this vicious cohabit my body without my ever knowing it? All my life I had had to deal with suppressed, controlled anger which I naturally thought was my problem. After this releasement, I realized that my anger had been provoked by my Dark Forces. Truly, the dark realm's method of control is very subtle and covert.

I took my new knowledge home and looked for people on whom to practice. This time the volunteers were even more scarce. Discarnates scared people enough. Dark Forces were more than most people could handle — not that I could blame them. The experience could be terribly frightening, and Dark Forces are definitely not nice guys. I have even had them threaten to kill my client if I didn't leave them alone. And this spoken through the client to me. Imagine the client's fear!

All in all, Baldwin's technique was revolutionary, but it still had limitations. Dark Forces are much less willing to show themselves and communicate than are discarnates. Also, their personalities are so terrible that the client frequently becomes emotionally exhausted by the time their session is over. Rarely could more than one Dark Force be released in a session, so several sessions were usually required. I personally had private sessions later with the Baldwins to have more releasement work done on myself. The cost was $300 for a two-hour session. I felt this fee was prohibitive to too many people who needed this work. I simply wasn't satisfied. I wanted to find an affordable, less traumatic way of releasing these beings.

In the meantime, my mental and psychic abilities continued to blossom. I was able to "go into" different animals, plants, minerals and experience their existence, and in the case of animals, their deaths. I also experienced my own higher Self as a huge angelic-type being, powerful, loving and omnipotent. It was this latter experience that anchored in me the understanding of this third-dimensional illusion. There was nothing to be afraid of and nothing that could harm me. Certainly, some blobs of intelligent black energy, which Dark Forces are, were no threat at all to my true essence. I discovered that I had the ability to communicate with other forms of intelligence — nature spirits, devas and animals. Not only did I converse with Andronymous, but with various angelic beings and ascended Masters as well. It came as no surprise therefore, when I met a healer who suggested that I communicate with the intelligence of human organs. What a wonderful concept! If I could speak to the intelligence of just about anything, why not to a human cell? It made a lot of sense.

I experimented on myself one night by speaking to my breast cysts which had plagued me all of my adult life. I thanked them for being the wonderful co-creative intelligence that they were and for providing a learning lesson for me. But, if I had learned the lesson and the lesson no longer served me, would they please leave? They said, "Yes," and the next morning my cysts were gone. I had come upon something new and wonderful!

Over months, with the help of this healer, my spiritual guidance and my medical knowledge, I expanded this concept to include all forms of physical dysfunction. A new world of learning opened to me. The intelligences within clients discussed with me how they felt and why, what effect they had had on the client, what they were trying to accomplish, and much more. What struck me the most was the importance and sensitivity of every cell — each one having a purpose and consciousness, and longing to be recognized for the role that it played. With help from my inner guidance, I evolved this technique and named it Cellular Memory Release. My clients' results have been profound.

I found that I moved very well within these other dimensions, so much so that it was easier for me to do healings alone, in an altered state, than to have the client in front of me. Always working with my spiritual guidance, I would find their soul/mind fragmentations and reintegrate them. I could see their etheric and astral bodies, and with the spiritual team with whom I work, discover implants and parasitic energies that we would remove.

Once, during a remote Cellular Memory Release session, I suddenly saw six Dark Forces staring at me from within my client's energy field. They were glaring at me with such threatening malice that I felt certain they were going to attack me any second. Caught totally off guard, I was considering what to do next, when a huge, flaming blue sword came down between them and me. Archangel Michael then instructed me on how to proceed with the session. Using a combination of Bill Baldwin's techniques and Archangel Michael's instructions, each of the Dark Forces were escorted to the Light along with all of the client's discarnates. With my subsequent clients, Archangel Michael and the Masters worked with me to perfect this new technique. At last, a kind way to remove the Dark Forces with absolutely no trauma to the client! Also, all Dark Forces and all discarnates could be released in one session, greatly reducing the client's number of sessions and cost.

Over time, I became used to Michael's sword coming down between my clients and me whenever I encountered Dark Forces. During one particular session, however, instead of the sword coming down between the client and myself, the sword was handed to me and I was told that, from then on I would "wear it." I then saw two swords, one in front of me and one behind me, suspended and permanently anchored in my aura, and heard Michael say, "You are now my warrior."

FROM OUT THE TURBULENT WATERS

The soul's dark cottage, battered and decayed,
Lets in new light through chinks that time has made.
Stronger by weakness, wiser men become,
As they draw near to their Eternal home.

— Edmund Waller, *Verses Upon His Divine Poesy*

Again, in my numerological ninth year, I left Florida for the high mountains of Arizona. Back to the clean air and my beloved pine trees, for a much needed physical and spiritual rest. I was informed that my ultrasound career was over and that I would have the opportunity to dedicate myself full-time to spiritual service. Such has proven to be true. And I finally figured it all out! I never did let the bastards get me down, did I?

For all the pain, I have to say that it's been a most wonderful life which I wouldn't trade with anyone. The rewards for enduring have far surpassed the suffering. And what of my parents? The wounds between us finally healed. It takes tremendous work to heal the resentment that can be created within a family, but when one dedicates oneself to self-growth, the Universe obliges and "miracles" occur. That I could have loved my parents or understood them then as I do now! But we were all three children engulfed in life's illusions, trying to raise ourselves in this most bitter of worlds.

Nothing happens by accident, nor are any of us victims. Prior to incarnation we plan our lives, both to clear our karmic debts and to prepare us for our particular life purpose. Frequently the very energies that we need to fulfill our purpose as adults, are the very ones that were so oppressive to us as children. By way of explanation, I refer to my own astrological natal chart. You need not thoroughly understand astrology to grasp the following points. Simply understand that I, as did all of you, chose to be born under the planetary alignments that best sup-ported my needs for this incarnation. As unpleasant as the energies from these alignments may appear, they serve their purpose. Once we swim from out the turbulent waters, stand dry on the shore and see the ocean, we find that it is a beautiful sight, indeed!

The sun was in the constellation of Pisces when I was born. The planets Pluto and the Moon are ascending in Leo, the first house sign, in which I declare my basic personality-body complex. The gentle, intuitive Pisces on the inside was masked by the strong, aggressive outward appearance of Leo. It was this mask behind which I hid most of my life to protect my oversensitive emotions. Not only was Leo a mask I used as a child, but eventually its leadership and power meld-ed with my Pisces nature, integrating those qualities and endowing me with the power to stand strong against my opposition, seen or unseen.

With Scorpio in the 4th house cusp (representing father and the inner world) I have the ability to move into the hidden realms. Scorpio brings extremes, nega-tive or positive. When the negative Scorpio influences are transmuted, they come into the higher aspects such as healing, work of a psychic nature and positive influences over the dark realms. With Pluto in the 1st house and ruler of the 4th house, and with the Sun, Mercury and Venus in Pisces, I am given the ability to access the inner realms, moving back and forth through the veil easily, and am given power over the Dark Forces and hidden esoteric things. But what agony I endured from the dark realms while I learned to consciously understand and work within them! Had it not been for the positive use of these planetary aspects I may well have been swallowed by darkness. On the other hand, had it not been for them, I probably would not have encountered these realms at all. Pluto also shows defiance which gave me the strength to stand firm, keeping my integrity within the dark realms, whereas my Sun, Venus and Mercury in my 8th house of Pisces, indicative of the hidden subconscious realm, gives me the ability to be sen-sitive to them. This speaks of the ability to deal with unseen and psychic forces and either eliminate or transmute them.

In my 3rd house, associated with school life, neighbors, and family, I have Saturn and Neptune in Libra. This indicates limitation, oppression, not getting along with others and total confusion and discord with associates and inner feel-ings. Without a doubt, this was my experience well into my adult life. But as with all negative aspects in my natal chart, I was, to a large degree, able to transmute them and use them in a positive way. These unpleasant experiences have empow-ered me with understanding and enabled me to work with the spiritually unaware mind in others. Along with the intuition and sensitivity of Pisces, I have these strong planetary influences which now enable me to assist those with con-fused minds attain their spiritual goals.

The aspects between the planetary positions mentioned here further qualify the nature of their influences on me, but are too numerous to mention.

Now, please do not run and check your natal chart to see if you have enough influences supporting you to do interdimensional work. If you are seriously interested in doing this type of work, you are supported. Also understand that I came here not only to understand and conquer the other realms, but to organize and teach my findings to others. Therefore, being a leader and forerunner (Pluto ascending in Leo), I have more planetary influences supporting me in these areas than might be the occasional user of these interdimensional techniques. Your influences will support your main life purpose.

Astrologically, my natal chart substantiates my life experiences in this third dimensional plane. I would now like to share with you a channeling that I received from St. Germain in which he sums up my interdimensional work and intergalactic origin as seen from a greater, spiritual perspective.

"... Would you like more information as to your responsibilities in this incarnation? Then let me help you. You, as you know, are a representative of our galactic organization. You have often staffed our mighty starships both in this galaxy and in others. Our ships and other realms are nothing new to you. In this life you are still ambassador for us. You represent not only our intergalactic fleet of ships and beings, but also your own form of sentient life. You, dear one, would be surprised at the forms that you have taken in your past. This helps make you so understanding of different races and people on the earth now. You have always represented varying life forms and have always been a herald for equality, though there have been times in your evolution that you were not so considerate, but this is long in the past. On, now, to your present assignment. Your function is a very mighty one. You did not choose to assist in a small, or what might appear to you as insignificant way. Little do you see the grandeur of your work. Dear one, you have come to aid at the deepest core level of healing. The very core of darkness you have taken upon yourself to remove. This comes from so many lifetimes of varying forms of battle, as you have conquered and brought light to many planets and realms in your eons of galactic and stellar work. As stated, you have not always been kind to these varying forms that you have met. In fact, in your zeal, you have behaved harshly. Realize that this was long ago, and now, for many eons, you have made retribution by embracing in your bosom all forms of life and sentient beings. How many are understanding the concept of unity of all life? How many appreciate all life, sentient forms, intelligences, like you do? In your desire to be of service, you have even well understood the sentient intelligence of darkness. Who better than you to herald this understanding to the sleeping masses? Even the light workers themselves are in grave ignorance of the darker pining of this planet and the invisible realms. Blessed Shakura, look at the sacrifice you have made to accept the path of supposed danger to the way of the underworld. Armed with your strength and love for all, yes, even the darkness, you volunteer to bring all to the light. Know that there are others who, like you, do work which very few are able or willing to take upon themselves. Yes, even in the higher realms, before incarnation, many chose to leave this work to others who were more capable. This is why you have undertaken this journey. . . ."

To all who have taken upon themselves the position of spiritual warrior, I salute, honor and bless you. May the baring of my soul, by means of this autobiography, bring you strength and understanding in whatever form of spiritual work you may pursue.

With blessings and love — I AM Shakura Rei

PART II

THE SPIRITUAL WARRIOR

There are more things in heaven and earth, Horatio,
than are dreamt in your philosophy.

— William Shakespeare, *Hamlet*

ASCENSION/TRANSMUTATION

Sincerity of conviction and purity of motive
will surely gain the day.
And even a small minority armed with these
is surely destined to prevail against all odds.

— Swami Vivekananda

It is very possible that some of you reading this have had an inner feeling that this is your last life on earth. There is a reason for that: For many of you it is. We are living in wondrous times indeed on this planet, with a grand experience in store for all of us. We are active participants in the birthing of a new Light planet Earth and a new Light species of humans.

Throughout this book I mention the Earth's "ascension" or "transmutation." It appears that most Light workers have a sense of this process, but the specifics elude them. The term "ascension," when applied to Earth and mankind, is relatively new. It was mentioned about fifty years ago by the Master Djwhal Khul in his channelings through Alice Bailey. He also described the spiritual initiations that evolving humans experience as they journey beyond the need for further embodiments, ultimately leading to the process of ascension. Other than Djwal's writings, Earth has seen a few examples of ascension, the best known being that of the Christ. Probably the most recent internationally known and viewed ascension was that of Paramahansa Yogananda who, in 1952, standing before an audience, raised his arms heavenward and consciously left his body. As evidence of this miraculous act, his physical form showed no signs of decay for twenty-one days. Most of us, however, believe that ascension is only achieved by people who are far more "evolved" than us — we feel they must embody "superior qualities" while we consider ourselves ordinary people, simply trying to do our best. So why all the talk these days about ascension; what is it and how does it relate to us?

Let's go back to basics. I am going to take a very complicated concept and oversimplify it for the purpose of explanation. My apologies to Madam Blavatsky and the Mystery Schools for any liberties taken on their very thorough and specific teachings on cosmology and the creation and evolution of mankind.

Consider Source — the creator of all that is. Consider Source prior to creation, as a mass of consciousness, limitless and without boundaries, with no life forms or intelligence outside of *itself*. At some point Source decided to experience all the possibilities of *itself*. To do so, it *individualized* parts of itself so that it could experience on a greater level. To do so, Source began to vibrate and create from its being seven great Rays, each Ray having its own distinct attributes yet remaining a form of Source.

An analogy might be a wave to the ocean. The wave is the ocean and yet it is slightly individualized because it is a "wave." After creating the Rays, Source chose to individualize even more. What could it, in the form of the Rays, accomplish? To find out, the rays themselves vibrated and created, each creation being an individualized essence of that Ray. One individualization, or intelligence as we might call it, was the monad. The monad also chose to experience itself, but in the most minute detail. What would it be like to experience duality? Pain? Struggle? Individualization to the point of apparent separation from its own Self? Because monad (Ray/Source) vibrates so quickly and is so pure, it is not able to experience density in its present form. Instead, it slows (or "steps down") its energies and essence to create what has been called the soul. Again it steps down, this time into the dense physical structure, and finally into personality/ego. The ego experiences individualization of the greatest form as witnessed by most of humans who have no awareness of their greater Self but consider the personality/ego the totality of their being.

Source experiences its own potential through the Rays, which in turn experience themselves through various creations such as the monad, which experiences through the soul, the physical form and then the ego. Understand then, that each human is composed entirely of Source, as all-that-is is created from Its being. However, the human feels separate from Source because his Source or God-essence has been individualized again and again. Each step of this individualization process produces a sense of separation. Again, using the analogy of the ocean, we can individualize the ocean to a wave. The wave fills a crevice in a rock and becomes a pool of water, then spilling out and becoming drops of water. Would a drop of this water believe itself to be the ocean? Perhaps not. It has been individualized so many times that it has now taken a form quite different from its beginning. However, what is its essence? The same as the ocean's, is it not? In the same manner we can liken ourselves, embodied physical humans, to our original essence — Source.

Over lifetimes the human ego begins to weary of being so alone — feeling so separate — and begins to yearn for a greater understanding of itself. As this yearning strengthens, the personality becomes aware (though not always consciously) of its soul. Then begins an integration of the personality and soul. As the soul is of a higher vibration, it raises the lower vibration of the physical form and increases the understanding of the personality by dominating it, taking over where the ego, with its sense of separation, once ruled. Now the soul also wishes to return to its Source, so as the human is influenced by the soul, he finds himself striving even harder towards Self and spiritual knowing. Here begins the integration of the monad, and eventually the integration of Source. Understand that the human, at this point, has not *become* the soul or monad, but has integrated their qualities.

The processes of integration have been referred to as spiritual initiations. When one has reached the level of initiation at which the soul no longer needs to experience duality within dense matter, one has ascended. Understand, however, that ascension is not a one-time event, nor is it an end. Ascension is merely "ascending" or stepping up from one level to another. In the case of Earth, we refer to it as ascending to a level in which we need no longer incarnate. This, in the past, has been called the achievement of "mastery." But after that we still have far to go. Our possibilities for experience are limitless! It has been said that there are 352 initiations between Earth experience and merging back into Source. To ascend without a further requirement for physical Earth incarnations one need only reach the level of the fifth and sixth initiations. Needless to say, we have much ahead of us!

There is a slight difference between ascension available for us today and that which has been experienced in the past. Prior to the Harmonic Convergence of 1987, when the Earth began her movement into the fourth dimension, those who reached a point of spiritual integration referred to as the fifth and sixth initiations, dropped the physical body and continued their evolution and Earth service as disembodied "ascended Masters." Due to the amount of Light that their body absorbed, their physical form, for the most part, could not maintain so high of a vibration and death of the physical was required. Paramahansa Yogananda's mahasamadhi, or conscious exit of his physical body in 1952, was an example of this process. At that time, Swami Yogananda became an ascended Master. He now serves Earth from the plane in which he dwells.

However, his process of ascension differed somewhat from that which is available to us now. As we are entering the fourth dimension and vibrating more quickly, we are able to hold greater amounts of Light, pass our fifth and sixth initiations and remain embodied.

One might wonder why, if we have integrated so much of our divine Self, have such great spiritual awareness and abilities, and can carry tremendous quantities of Light, would we want to remain on this planet of duality and pain? The answer is *service*. As one integrates more of one's soul, monadic and Source levels, the ego's illusion of separation melts away and is replaced by the consciousness of unity and oneness with all things. One does not only understand on a mental level, but one experiences within one's being the Divine within all life. At that point, one has progressed from self consciousness to group consciousness, where there is no longer an attitude of "Beam me up, Scottie" (or Ashtar). Therefore, one has become immersed in the desire to assist others in furthering their spiritual advancement. Certainly there is much service available to us from the ascended Masters, angelic realm and space brothers and sisters. These, however, are all limited as to the extent of help that they can offer us. It takes a physical form to physically get things accomplished. That is why the Light workers of today are desperately needed to assist in healing each other and the Earth. The time for this has come. Understand that those of us who are consciously serving the Light and working towards ascension are heading home. We are completing the last mile of our Earth journey. Coming from a high level of integration, we become aware that though we may individually ascend, from a greater perspective we are ascending as a group. We are part of a mass consciousness and soul group, and we desire to assist all who choose to move towards the same goal: global ascension never before experienced by the Adamic human, and a quantum leap in our spiritual evolution. Due to the new vibrations on the planet, more and more people are ascending but remaining here to continue their chosen life assignment.

To ascend, one integrates one's wholeness. In so doing the Lightbody is formed. As we move into a different dimension, naturally we must dwell within a different dimensional body. The Lightbody is not composed of atoms as is our dense physical body, nor is it to be confused with the astral body. Rather it is the body created by the merging of our Selves and is composed of Light particles referred to as microtrons. As the microtron permeates each atom, it accelerates the physical and creates the Lightbody. With the vibratory rate of the physical body increasing, the Light within each atom grows brighter as it releases its physical density.

Ascension is now possible for *all* of mankind and not just the very few, because the Earth has left the third dimension and vibrates much higher and more quickly than it did. Therefore, the higher vibrations can more easily integrate with what was once too dense a structure. The process of raising the vibrations higher as we go deeper into the fourth dimension is called transmutation. The dense atomic cellular structure of matter is literally transmuting into Light. We don't visually see a difference in structure because, for the most part, everything is transmuting within the same range of frequency. Therefore everything appears the same as we are all expanding in a parallel fashion.

The process of transmutation is something that is happening whether we want it to or not. It always precedes ascension. We have no free will in this matter other than to take the course of physical death. Everything upon and within this planet is experiencing transmutation as we move deeper into the fourth, and eventually into the fifth dimensions. Ascension, however, is a conscious choice.

I might add that transmuting is not a particularly enjoyable thing. When the cells of our body mutate and change form, they go into a state of temporary stress and imbalance which manifests as various physical symptoms. The greater the transmuting, the greater is the imbalance. This is why self-healing is imperative at this time. The more we clear ourselves of dense energies, the smoother the transmutation process will be for us. It's likely that everyone reading this has experienced some form of transmutation symptoms, the most common being exhaustion. For no reason of which you are aware, you may find yourself sleeping up to twelve hours a day but still feeling tired. You may experience this for a few weeks or a few months; it tends to come and go. Other signs of transmutation are a desire to find inner peace, to be out of the rat race, and a greater feeling of oneness with everyone and everything. You might also notice your feelings becoming more intense. Anger, for example, may surface with a vengeance, both to your horror and surprise. Perhaps you'll become very emotional and cry for no apparent reason. Many old, suppressed issues may surface for you to look at and release. You may notice body aches and pains, flu-like symptoms, or have the feeling that your body is detoxifying.

Something that almost everyone is aware of is the sense that time is speeding up. In actuality, time is imploding upon itself. There is "no time" in the higher dimensions, and as we go deeper into the fourth and eventually into the fifth dimension, linear time gradually disappears. In the present linear time, we are currently experiencing approximately fifty minutes per sixty minute hour. For that reason, what we think or choose to create also manifests quicker, be it a positive thought or a harmful one.

If you are working on ascension and integrating your Selves, you may notice radical changes in your belief system. As you integrate a higher awareness and understanding, you may find that what you once believed is no longer true for you; your truth actually changes as you become aware of higher concepts. These concepts often come as a "knowing" that has been integrated during your sleep. You may wake up one morning with an understanding of a particular topic that is different from the understanding you had the day before. It's as if you woke up and suddenly "got it." The more one integrates, the more one "gets it," the more one's belief system is in an upheaval. Eventually you may become so inundated with a constantly changing "knowing," that you may go into a state of overwhelm and shut down for a while. It is at that point one feels as if *I know so much that I am totally convinced that I don't know a thing!* Here you may begin a temporary withdrawal from meditating, active service or spiritual striving. Rest assured that this is only temporary and doesn't mean that you have lost all interest in your spiritual growth. It is merely a period of integration and rest from all this transmutation upheaval. In all likelyhood, you'll be ready to strive forward again within a few weeks. This process of constantly changing "knowing" explains why truth can never be a concrete reality.

We experience our truth according to our understanding. I am reminded of the question about the unnoticed tree falling in the woods. If it was not part of anyone's experience — no one saw, heard, thought of or in any way knew of its falling — did it really fall? In whose reality is this fallen tree a truth? I would have to say, *no one's*. However, if I had walked by the tree and saw it fall, then it would become part of my truth, but not yours. If I later emphatically stated that the tree fell, you may, through our energetic connection, also begin to believe that it fell. Eventually my reality may become yours. And so it is as we become more aware and expansive.

Understand that ascension is part of our spiritual evolution and will eventually occur for everyone. It's just a matter of time. Some of my clients have stated that this whole concept of leaving Earth for "realms unknown" is scary to them. Though they consider themselves Light workers and on a spiritual path, they do not consciously seek ascension. In addressing this attitude, let me state that the Lightbody will be *the* body for the New Age of Earth. Eventually we will all ascend beyond the need for physical embodiment — either now or later, on this planet or another. It would behoove us to strive for that goal now, while so much opportunity is available.

Ascension is a point within our spiritual growth, and with all growth there must be a certain amount of striving and will, without which we would remain stagnant. It can be stated that all will spiritually grow at one time or another because the cosmos is in a state of constant flux. Nothing remains still indefinitely, and that includes the circumstances and attitudes of every individual. However, from Earth's perspective, understand that without will and dedication, one may remain stagnant for a very long time. By dedication, I not only refer to the desire to grow spiritually, awaken to truth and transcend the present illusion of the Earth plane, but also a dedication to heal one's self on all levels of one's being.

For example, if one has a nagging fear of ascension, then recognize "fear" as an emotion which holds the self in limitation, being part of the third-dimensional illusion of separation from one's total divine Self. The next appropriate step would be to remove the fear. In this case "fear" represents a block, or a hindrance, in the form of cellular memory. It is a fog before an individual's eyes, distorting the truth he is trying to perceive. Throughout our numerous incarnations, we humans have accumulated many such blocks. Most blocks take the form of parasitic energy attachments, negative thoughtforms, dark energies stored in the cells, and one's every day self-created emotional "stuff." Think of these blocks as smog in each person's aura. We'll call this smoggy person "A." Now person A meets person B. Not only must A see through his own smog, but he must also look through B's smog in his attempt to see or perceive B. In other words, A is seeing through the dark filters of his own negativity, biases and concepts, as well as those projected by B. So how clearly does the average person see or perceive the truth? Pretty scary, isn't it?

This is why we must take responsibility for ourselves and clear the blocks. Certainly, we are often at a loss as to how to overcome a certain attitude or physical condition. A healer may well have the tools that we are in need of, but remember that a healer heals no one. One always heals one's self; the healer merely assists. Healing begins with introspection and realization that there are attitudes that need to be resolved. From there one must make a firm dedication to resolve or transmute them. When that dedication is directed to the Universe, the healing will occur. One occasionally finds that the attitude or condition is still serving a purpose and is not yet ready to be transmuted. Whatever the case may be, nothing can be accomplished without first desiring and then willing that desire into action.

There are also those who feel that they will ascend one way or the other and therefore assume an attitude of indifference towards their self-healing, taking little responsibility for their spiritual progress. They assume that they may sit back and wait for the Universe to bless them with ascension. They will be sitting for a very long time! They will sit until they have acquired the needed will and responsibility for their own growth, at which point the Universe will assist them, but only in proportion to their dedication. "Enlightenment" will not be handed to anyone on a silver platter!

Those individuals who choose not to take an active role in their self-healing may not be able to withstand the higher resonance of the fourth and fifth dimensions. As their cells attempt to fill with more Light, there will be resistance by the dense energies the cells still contain. The resulting imbalance can cause pain in a literal sense — both emotional and physical. In such a state, not only may serious illness be created, but negative emotions contained within the cells may surface: anger, hate, jealously, fear, prejudice, or any number of other harmful pathos. Unlike those who choose to transmute such energies, these individuals may remain locked into their emotions. Therefore many of them will leave the Earth through death and continue their evolution on another third-dimensional planet which is more compatible with their present state of vibration and consciousness. I would like to add that an understanding attitude towards the spiritually unaware is important. Such people are not "less than" or undeserving in some way. Understand that not all humans have been experiencing Earth life for the same length of time. Some of us have been here a very long time while others are fairly young as incarnated humans. These have been referred to as old and young souls. For the most part, the older souls are the ones who are creating their Lightbodies, working towards ascension and releasing their karma. This is because they have experienced all that they need in order to complete their human journey. What is left for them now is to transcend the veils of illusion and embrace their Selves. The younger souls, however, are still experiencing. Remember, on a higher level we all came here to *experience*. We did it on purpose; we thought it would be a fun trip. For those people who are still experiencing and still have experiences ahead of them, it would be unjust to take that away. However, they won't be able to remain on Earth because Earth will no longer permit third dimensional situations and attitudes. These people must eventually leave, one way or the other, and continue their third dimensional journey somewhere else. So, when you hear of mass deaths from Earth changes, disease, and various other calamities, know that a kindness is actually being extended.

The energies that are now anchoring into Earth are due to five new cosmic Rays. These Rays are bringing about the energy of the New Age, thus making ascension a possibility on a global level for all who desire that course. For those of you who do not understand the first seven Rays or their significance, I suggest reading *The Rays and the Initiations* by Djwhal Khul, channeled through Alice Bailey.

The following is a brief synopsis of the five additional Rays:
- **Ray 8** is a green-violet cleansing ray, composed of the 4th, 5th and 7th Rays. It is excellent for cleansing and balancing the emotional body.
- **Ray 9** is a blue-green combination of Rays 1 and 2. This Ray initiates the process of breaking the bonds to the physical plane by establishing soul contact. It also initiates the association with the Lightbody.
- **Ray 10** is pearl-white, containing the 1st, 2nd, and 3rd Rays. It is the Ray that actually builds and encodes the Lightbody, integrates all levels of Self, and speeds us through our initiations.
- **Ray 11** is an orange-pink blend of the 1st, 2nd and 5th Rays. This Ray assists the advent of the New Age and removes the remnants of third-dimensional energies that are no longer applicable.
- **Ray 12** is golden and combines all Rays. It brings the energies from the Source level and is the highest form of energy presently available on Earth. It will raise the vibration of anything towards which it is directed.

For more information on these five new Rays, I suggest the book, *Evolution, Our Loop of Experiences*, by Janet McClure.

The new rays integrate into our system by entering through the central channel, also known as the Rainbow Bridge or Antakarana. This does not imply that they are *limited* to entering through this channel. All rays can impart their qualities by showering the entire body and auric field; however, the five new rays are particularly useful for building the Lightbody, and pass through the central channel for this purpose. According to Djwhal, this tubular channel is approximately one-fourth inch wide in the average human, extending from our physical form down into the Earth and up through cosmic universes. As we integrate more of our spiritual identity, remove our blocks and develop our Lightbody, this channel widens. Most active Light workers have channels from two to four inches wide. This, however, is just the beginning. Ideally, the channel can expand beyond our body, radiating out from us like our aura. I assure you that this is not difficult to accomplish once one understands how to work with the five new rays. With sincere desire and will, while using the following techniques, one's channel can be expanded to encompass an area much larger than one's body. One can achieve a strong, well-developed Lightbody and integrate beyond the sixth initiation, all within months to a couple year's time. The time factor would depend on one's spiritual starting point and the strength of one's determination.

When we were deep within the third dimension, we were not able to vibrate within the sixth initiation and remain incarnate. As we moved into the fourth dimension, it was channeled that we could integrate to the seventh initiation, but not further while remaining incarnate. As of this writing, we no longer have any of these restrictions. There also used to be a limit as to how much Light we could carry while embodied. All the rules have now changed. To illustrate, we could say that the Adamic human had a potential that ranged from one to one hundred. Such a limit existed because the density and condition of this planet did not permit potentials beyond a certain range. Since Earth has now entered a new paradigm and all the rules have changed, the end point of human potential is now unknown. Individually, many of us have greatly surpassed the previous limit of one hundred, and have already ascended but are remaining embodied to bring to conclusion our chosen Earth assignments.

Understand that ascension is not a waking-up one morning and finding oneself perfect. Rather it is a process of gradual integration, gaining more spiritual insight, seeing the illusion of the personality and the roles that it has played, knowing, experiencing, and then *being* the oneness with all that is. Divine, unconditional love replaces the old programming of jealousy, fear, and ethnic, religious and national separatism as well as separation from one's Self. The ascended person becomes transformed, and who she once was is no longer who she is now. Her history no longer applies other than to be the building blocks for what she has become. The ascended being also carries huge amounts of Light which can be felt, seen or sensed by those who come into her contact. Gradually, as more integration occurs and more dense energies are transmuted, what will be seen as the physical body will also reach a point of perfection as it blends and integrates totally with the Lightbody.

Those of you who are aligned with the space brothers and sisters and the Ashtar Command may be under the impression that your ascension will occur over a few days' time on the ship. I have asked Ashtar about this and he has repeatedly assured me that ascension is a gradual process and is not instantly accomplished. However, the process can be assisted on the ships. There are, at various locations on and off the planet, ascension seats or chambers, one being on the Ashtar Command. These are places where we may go during sleep to have our bodies healed or "Lightened" up. After we have reached the point of integration referred to as ascension, then we may be helped to learn teleportation, invisibility, instantaneous manifestation, and other processes, on the ships. The concept of actually *ascending* on the ships came from channeled information years ago. It went hand-in-hand with a proposed mass lift-off. During the lift-off, as a reward for their service, many of those evacuated would be accelerated through to their ascension. This had been proposed only if conditions on Earth were such that global death appeared imminent. As I write this, the space crew feel that the Light is presently anchoring very well on Earth. Ascension is occurring now, and the past prophecies of gloom, doom and destruction no longer apply. Although Earth will continue to shake, tremble and erupt as she cleans herself, the consequences of her cleansing will not be nearly as traumatic as has been predicted by Nostradamus or the Book of Revelations, for example.

While on the topic of the space command, I must digress somewhat. All incarnated humans have a lineage; we were somewhere and did something before we came to Earth. In this era, as we prepare to return "home," many of us are becoming aware of that lineage. Those who resonate strongly with E.T.'s, especially a particular group, were probably of, or strongly affiliated with that group before incarnating. I have heard stories from many people who have had various forms of loving contacts with E.T.'s. The E.T.'s remind them of their heritage; they are their forgotten family and are here to welcome them home from their Earth journey. As an extraterrestrial group contacts their Earth members, certain arrangements or provisions may have been made for them. The provisions may vary from group to group, which is why they don't necessarily ring true for each and every Light worker. I feel this is the case with the Ashtar Command. Many of us receive information that doesn't seem to apply to other Light workers. My personal opinion is that most of that information is directed to those from a starship background. As this type of information is published it smacks of untruth to those not aligned with the Command. However, for others it confirms feelings or information that they may have already received. For this reason, it is wise to remember not to give your power away to channels or channeled material. Feel the truth in your heart and go with that.

What I have written about ascension applies to every incarnate human, regardless of whether they are part of the Command, Pleiadians, Arcturians, or any other known or unknown group. Remember, we are integrating our Selves. Your Self knows what is true and right for you. Be with that and flow with it as your truth becomes based on greater and greater awareness.

Let's now return to the five new rays, and also ray seven. These are the core "movers and shakers" that remove our accumulated smog and activate our Lightbody.

The following are suggestions for using these rays: You will want to call the rays to you. This is accomplished by focusing your attention on the ray and asking it to come to you. You can visualize the ray, call its name, or simply have a strong feeling for it. Each of these three ways is drawing energy towards it and getting its attention. This process of focusing energy to achieve an outcome is known as "intention." Perhaps you have created your intention, but are not sure if it was successful. In that case, the following analogy may be helpful. Create your intention and send it out into the ethers, as if it were following an etheric telephone wire. When you have a sense that someone picked up the telephone at other end, you are successful. It may feel as if "someone" received your call, or you may notice a slight shift of energy.

I'll begin with the **Seventh Ray** as it has been integral in accelerating us to the point of readiness for the other five.

The **Seventh Ray** is violet and has been called the Ray of Ceremonial Magic. Many people identify it with St. Germain and the violet flame. Indeed, St. Germain is the master of this ray. The violet flame is transmuting. I have used it for years in healing work on myself and others, and for transmuting "dirty" energy. Further in this book I discuss what to do with dirty energy, but for now simply know that it is not enough to just toss it in the corner; we need to transmute it to a higher form. Dirty energy remains dirty, free to recontaminate and pollute the etheric environment unless it is altered to a higher frequency, which can be accomplished by using the violet flame of the **Seventh Ray**. To use this ray on yourself, assume a meditative attitude. Visualize a huge violet flame permeating you and extending out at least six feet. If one sits within the flame for at least ten minutes each day, there will be a marked increase in the cleanliness of the aura as existing auric debris is gradually transmuted. If doing energy work on someone else, imagine the violet flame near you and throw the polluted energies into it.

To use the **Eighth Ray**, assume your meditative attitude, call in the **Eighth Ray** and feel it clean and balance your emotional body. Follow this process by sitting within the **Seventh Ray**'s violet flame to transmute any unclean energies that you have released.

If you are just consciously beginning to integrate your soul and activate the Lightbody, you will want to sit within the **Ninth Ray**. In your meditative state, call the **Ninth Ray**. As you feel its energy flowing around you and through your central channel, have the intention of breaking the limiting attitudes that hold you captive to the physical form. Then ask for development of your Lightbody as you call your soul to enter your central channel and integrate with you. Sit in this energy for awhile.

I will describe the Tenth Ray last, because it is the ray for building the Lightbody, integration and ascension.

The **Eleventh Ray** is good to direct toward the entire Earth as well as to yourself. It helps clear the remaining attitudes and conditions of the old third dimensional system, making room for the Twelfth Ray and the New Age. The golden **Twelfth Ray** permeates all that it touches with the divine energies of Source. It is the highest form of energy presently available on Earth. To use these rays, see the **Eleventh Ray** as an orange/pink tornado. Through your intention, allow it to descend on the Earth from the cosmos. As it penetrates the Earth, have it penetrate you as well. Follow this with a golden tornado formed from the **Twelfth Ray**.

As you can see, some preliminary work must be done in order to activate the Lightbody. First one must have the *intention* to expand beyond one's limiting belief systems while removing the bars that imprison the personality/ego and hold one in a state of separation. Then one must have the *will* or *determination* to follow through on whichever healing techniques are necessary to release nonserving attitudes and stored memory of pain. As these are removed, more space is available for Light to anchor within the bodies, reducing the traumatic effects of healing crises while also speeding the integration of the Selves and building the Lightbody.

Next, one must *actively and consciously activate* the Lightbody with the assistance of the **Tenth Ray**. Of course, there are innumerable meditations and techniques which can be used to develop the Lightbody. Understand that if they work, it is because the **Tenth Ray** is involved in the process, whether one realizes it or not. The **Tenth Ray** makes integration of the Lightbody possible. In my experience, observing the progress of others as well as myself, nothing speeds one's evolution as dynamically and quickly as the following procedure employing the **Tenth Ray**. What I am speaking of is not pie-in-the-sky but a reality which can be achieved within months — beyond the once restricted number of initiations, and beyond the ability to hold a restricted quantity of Light. It is important to understand that *all the rules have changed!*

When one begins to integrate beyond soul and monad levels to Source, the changes within one's awareness become absolutely dynamic. It is at this level where all reality, as we have know it, shatters before our eyes and we clearly see it for the illusion that it is. The illusion is replaced with a level of peace and understanding never before experienced in our Adamic journey.

If you have never done any ascension work or have not yet integrated with your soul through your own process of spiritual awakening, you would want to use the **Ninth Ray** along with this **Tenth Ray** technique. The **Ninth Ray** will prepare you for integrating the soul and Lightbody. Call the **Ninth Ray** first, then follow with the **Tenth Ray** while also calling for your soul. As the **Tenth Ray** and your Self flow through you, simply sit and integrate. Assume an attitude of absorption. Remember, it's you coming back to you! It's awesome and it's wonderful! Just sit and absorb, absorb, absorb!

To make best use of the **Tenth Ray**, assume a meditative attitude, then call the archangels to assist. With the assistance of our higher Selves, these angels have agreed to embody the rays and integrate them into our chakras, thus building the Lightbody. Simply ask the angel to **"please embody this chakra, now."** As with all techniques in this book, wait until you sense that your request is answered before moving on to your next request. Call the following angels for the corresponding chakras:

• Crown and higher chakras — Archangel Metatron
• Third eye — Archangel Ratziel
• Throat/Thymus/Heart — Archangel Khamael
• Solar plexus — Archangel Michael
• Spleen — Archangel Raphael to the right
    — Archangel Gabriel in the center
    — Archangel Uriel to the left
    (they form a V shape with Raphael and Uriel at the top and Gabriel at the point)
• Root — Archangel Sandalphon

Now envision or direct your attention to your central channel. It is a tube extending from the cosmos, through the top of your head and down your spine, and finally deep into the center of the Earth. It is through this channel that you will pull the energies and consciousness of your soul, monad and Source levels into your physically manifested being. The central channel is also the site through which the **Tenth Ray** enters, taking these energies from your higher Selves to build your Lightbody.

Ask Archangel Sandalphon to pull Earth energies up your channel. Then ask Archangel Metatron to open your crown and higher chakras as wide as is safe. Call the **Tenth Ray** and feel it shower you with its energies. Your intention is that it continue to flow through you during this process. If you feel it slacken off, call it again. As the **Tenth Ray** is flowing, call your soul. Notice how much energy flows from it. Then call monad, then Source. Notice which has the stronger flow of energy. Whichever flows the strongest is what you are integrating at that time.

Because we presently think within a linear construct, I have described the above process implying that parts of you are "out there" and that you are pulling them back in. This is not actually correct but certainly helps explain the concept. The truth is that all your Selves are *within* you at this moment and also within the person next door, the tree in the yard, the tiger in India and the volcano in Hawaii. Your soul interpenetrates your physical being and is not a structure or identity separate from you, but rather an essence of your consciousness within you. Your monad and Source are also forms of your consciousness entwined within. They are all levels of your being, that have stepped down in energy/consciousness in order to create your personality and self-identity as you know it. What stops one from experiencing these levels of Self are veils of illusion — accumulated "smog." As you call to those parts of Self and the **Tenth Ray** to integrate and absorb with you, you are actually recognizing their existence. In essence you're saying, "O.K. I finally know you're here. How about we work as a team from now on!"

The higher Selves do not impose themselves upon the personality, rather they permit the personality (over the span of lifetimes) to experience its illusions and sense of separation. Once the personality recognizes that it has a soul, it endeavors to walk with that soul. Then the personality and soul continue this process with the monad and Source. So when we talk about integrating and absorbing, we are merely asking for the veils to be removed so that we can fully experience and be all aspects of our Selves. The removal of the veils is evidenced by the expansion of the central channel. Therefore healing, ascending, integrating Self, spiritual growth and the initiations are all based on the same principle, which is becoming and being all that you are, as a spiritual essence.

There are some things that you can do to accelerate the process of integration even more. The first few times you work with the **Tenth Ray**, it is valuable to educate the body consciousness as to what is going on. This is part of Cellular Memory Release and is explained in detail under that chapter, but I have included the following sample dialogue here. As you sit within the **Tenth Ray**, tune into your own essence. In other words, you're going to have a talk with your inner self. Read or state in your own words the following information. Once your body understands what your intention is, it will flow with the process.

• Speak to the DNA.

"I speak directly to the DNA and say that the time of separation and death is over. I ask that all twelve strands of the original DNA be reactivated and reintegrated to their original twelve-strand form and purpose, now. I ask that all memory of the separation of these strands be released now, from the submost atomic level and from all bodies."

The human species originally had a twelve-strand DNA, which was deactivated except for two strands. The new human species will have the twelve-strand DNA fully functioning again, and we begin this process by asking them to reintegrate. If you are interested in reading more about the DNA and chakras of the new human, I suggest *Bringers of The Dawn* by Barbara Marciniak.

• Speak to the pituitary gland.

"I speak directly to the pituitary gland. In the past I have chosen life and death on Earth. I chose this for the experiences that Earth had to offer, but the time for death is over now. I am healing and becoming perfect in all ways. I thank you for all the lessons you have permitted me to learn, and I thank you for all the service you have provided me, but now is the time to stop the death process. I ask you to reverse the death hormone to the life hormone, now. I ask you to align all my glands for rejuvenation and begin the rejuvenation process, now. I ask the pituitary to release from the submost atomic level and from all bodies, all pain, dysfunction and anything less tham divine perfection, now. I ask that the thread of consciousness be joined from the pituitary to the pineal, and that I be joined to my higher purpose."

• Speak to the thymus.

"I ask the thymus to release from the submost atomic level of all cells and from all bodies, all pain, dysfunction and anything less than divine perfection. I ask the thymus to remember its perfect form and function and return to that state, now."

• Speak to the glands, in general.

"I ask the glands to release from the submost atomic level and from all bodies, all pain, dysfunction and anything less than divine perfection. I ask all glands to align with rejuvenation, now."

• Speak to the eighth atom.

"I ask the eighth atom to release all pain, dysfunction and anything less than divine perfection from the submost atomic level of the cells and from all bodies, now."

The eighth atom holds the holographic blueprint of your makeup and distributes that information throughout your developing cells.

- Speak to the permanent atom.

"I ask the permanent atom to remember its perfect function and direct me to my divine purpose, now."

The permanent atom holds the blueprint for your experiences. You might consider it as a book which contains the theme of your existence.

- **"I ask the Lightbody to become active and strong, now."**

- **"I honor and thank all intelligences that have assisted in this process."**

This transmuting process can be done alone or in conjunction with Cellular Memory Release.

The larger and cleaner your chakras are, the more substance the angels have to work with while embodying the rays into them. Therefore creating the thymus and skull-base chakras would be of great benefit if you haven't already done so. Also keep the chakras clean. How to open, build, and clean the chakras is described later in "Opening the Chakras." As most people have never given their central channel a second thought, a lot of sludge may have accumulated within it. To clean it, envision a golden tornado enter the top of your channel. As the tornado passes through, state that **"all dark energies within my channel enter this tornado, now."** The gold will automatically transmute those energies.

You can also help widen your channel, which will permit greater amounts of energy to permeate. The channel will widen itself as you integrate more and more, but in the beginning, especially if it is very narrow, you might want to assist it a little. To accomplish this, see a golden energy enter at the top. See this energy more as a corkscrew than a tornado. As it screws down, it opens the channel a little wider. Beware! *Forcing* the channel open can cause the energy to surge, which you may not be ready to handle. It is similar to the reaction of the kundalini raising before the person's bodies are ready. I generally don't recommend opening the channel, but I do feel that it is safe if done under the guidance of your higher Selves, gently and without force.

If you'd like to have some fun, try sketching your energy field as you see it today. Date it, then sketch it again some months later for comparison. Here's a technique to try: Close your eyes and visualize yourself standing sideways in front of you. Now intend to see your chakras and see how far your chakras extend. Then open your eyes and draw them. Be really open and non-judgmental about this. If you have pre-conceived ideas about what you look like but find something different, you will probably be inclined to doubt what you're seeing.

So if you see that your root chakra is almost non-existent for example, rather than get upset, you could simply think, "Gee, isn't this interesting? No wonder I'm so spacy!"

Close your eyes again and look for your central channel. Unless you are far advanced in your integrations, it will not be wider than your head. Don't confuse it with your higher chakras, which will have a different shape. The channel is a definite tube that runs completely through your body, top to bottom. Draw that once you see it.

Then look for your aura. Unless you've been doing aura work on yourself, don't expect it to be perfectly egg-shaped and smooth. It may jag in here and bulge out there, or may appear non-existent in other places. You may also notice a lot of debris floating in it. Not to panic — this book describes, in great detail, how to create one terrific energy field. Take note of all that you see, draw it and date it. If you do not already sit in the violet flame, I suggest that you begin today, and continue on a daily basis. After sitting in the flame a few minutes, follow with the **Tenth Ray** exercise. Make this a mandatory part of your daily meditation. As you read this book you will undoubtedly practice some of the techniques on yourself, but even if you don't, draw yourself again in a month and don't doubt what you see. You will be wonderfully pleased!

If you tried to see your energy field and simply couldn't get a clear image, ask a friend to use her inner or outer clairvoyant vision to help you. It's even better to draw yourself and have someone else draw you as well. Then you have confirmation as well as a barometer with which to measure your advancement.

The greatest indicators of spiritual growth are the changes that occur within, but along with inner changes come physical healings and tremendous changes in the energy field. Monitoring these changes can be fun and rewarding. Be careful not to make this a competition, however, with yourself or anyone else. You see, you already *are* magnificent; you already *are* a master. You've just been playing a game called third dimension and now the game is almost over. It's simply a process of removing the veils of amnesia and illusion. Once gone, you realize that you never left your divine spiritual Selves; you merely didn't see them.

We cannot look at someone and judge their spiritual growth, because we are all equally divine, living behind veils. No competition there. And for those who want to be the first one on the block to ascend, ask yourself, *why?* What is the point, other than an ego that has not integrated group consciousness yet? As for competing to clear as quickly as possible, even with yourself — this, too, is folly. You have no idea of the magnitude of challenges or pain stored within the cells, that you or anyone else holds. Can you set a limit on yourself and say, "*I expect to be this clear by this time, or why isn't that person clearer by now?*" Of course not. Competition is part of the old paradigm and has no place within the new. Your veils will fall away and your Lightbody will build according to your intention. That's all there is to it.

In a nutshell, ascension and initiations involve becoming and "being" our true spiritual Selves. We do this by integrating with our higher Selves and building a new body with the help of the **Tenth Ray** and the archangels. The new body is called a Lightbody and is comprised of the energies and consciousness of our soul, monad and Source levels.

If a person only works with the **Tenth Ray** and does no other healing work, he will still advance, but his advancement will be slower. I strongly suggest that if you do nothing more for yourself, at least open all your chakras using the very effective techniques in this book. That would include the known seven chakras plus the ones below the feet, above the crown, and the thymus and skull-base chakras. In this book you will find many healing techniques that you can use on yourself and others. They all reach the very deepest layers of sludge that has accumulated through lifetimes of third-dimensional density. Understand that this density no longer serves us as the old paradigm of third dimension Earth is rapidly leaving. It would not be advisable to hold on to your past experiences nor your past feelings, concepts or attitudes that no longer apply. Let them go. Earth is heralding in new energies, and so must we if we are to keep up. So, friends, journey Earth is almost over as we have known it. This is why we are incarnated at this time; we chose to be around for the grand finale. We might as well all sit in the front row!

To activate and build the Lightbody, call the archangels to embody your chakras:
- Crown and higher chakras –– Archangel Metatron
- Third Eye — Archangel Ratziel
- Throat/Thymus/Heart — Archangel Khamael
- Solar plexus — Archangel Michael
- Spleen — Archangel Raphael to the right
    — Archangel Gabriel in the center
    — Archangel Uriel to the left
- Root — Archangel Sandalphon
- Ask Sandalphon to pull Earth's energies up your channel from the ground.
- Ask Metatron to open your crown and higher chakras as much as is possible and safe.
- Call the Tenth Ray.
- Call your soul, monad and Source levels to come through your channel and integrate with you.
- Educate the body consciousness, using the dialogue described.
- Constantly call the soul, monad, Source and Tenth Ray to keep the flow going.

- Absorb, absorb, absorb! Sit in this as long as you can, or until you feel you have saturated enough for the time being. Do this every day.

RAYS AND ATTUNEMENTS

Energy is Eternal Delight.

— William Blake

In the last chapter I mentioned the seven great Rays which hold the substance of creation. In the most simple of terms, this means that they have the ability to create from their essence. These rays, or energies, contain individualized qualities referred to as subrays. Each subray is intelligent, contains its own particular qualities, and is slightly individualized from the greater ray.

Many rays and subrays are being directed towards the planet for healing at this time. These rays assist the planet in general, but are also available to us specifically. We may consciously ask to be attuned to them and, as they have their own intelligence, once we are attuned they will provide us with a continuous flow of healing energy as they see appropriate. Attunement to a ray increases one's Light quotient by raising one's vibrations. It also creates a relationship between the receiver and the attuning energy or the Light being that represents the energy, anchors greater amounts of Light to the Earth, and assists in the healing and transmuting process for the receiver.

These attunements clear, resonate and align the chakra and meridian systems, clean the cells of debris, and raise the vibrations of the bodies. The bodies are then saturated with the very high energies of that particular ray or master. If the receiver's bodies are exceptionally toxic on any of its levels, a healing crisis may occur. We all have bodies that are imbalanced to certain degrees. Were we in total balance, we would be in perfect health, both emotionally and physically. Within our imbalance most of us have reached a state of stabilization, that is, we function well within our imbalance, hardly knowing that it even exists. When we begin to heal we create an imbalance to that stability, causing turmoil and what appears as illness. This turmoil is called a healing crisis. Eventually we return to some form of stability.

If this imbalance and stability could be measured, we would find that our bodies had reached a higher state of balance after the healing crisis than before. One might say that we have become more balanced within our imbalance. Though the outcome of a healing crisis is positive, we would wish to gain favorable results without the trauma of a crisis. We would desire to heal more gradually with the least amount of disruption to the body as possible. Therefore, I strongly recommend that before anyone receives these rays, he avoid adding any undue stress upon his body, either physically or emotionally. All drugs, unless medically necessary, should be avoided. A juice fast or any form of healing or meditation prior to the session would be advantageous. Use common sense and be your own judge, understanding that receiving the rays can be very powerful. Some rays may vibrate you intensely, while others may feel like a puff of love surrounding you. Or you may just have a sense of "something happening" but be unable to define what that is.

Along with certain ray attunements, we may be attuned to the energy of certain ascended Masters. We can always ask for a blessing from the higher realms and we will receive it. Some of the masters will perform actual healings on us, during which they connect us energetically to themselves. Once this connection is established, there begins a certain amount of overshadowing from them, with the line of communication and assistance always open.

Not all attunements are available to everyone, for some are dependent upon the discretion of the attuning master. Rest assured that this is not a case of playing favorites. Those attunements that are discretionary may be thought of as rewards, or initiations into higher realms of consciousness. Although I am sure that almost everyone reading this book is on a dedicated healing and awakening journey, some are further along the path than others. If you feel you may be one of the newcomers, please do not limit yourself. Time is speeding up so incredibly fast that what would have taken a few years for a quantum leap in consciousness is now taking but a few months.

Attunements may be done physically, which means that a person who is already attuned, may pass that attunement on to you through certain physical ceremony. An attunement may also be done etherically, from the "inner" levels, in which case a being who is in spirit, usually a master or angel, attunes you directly. Both forms of attunements may have certain drawbacks. If choosing to be attuned in the physical, you first must find an individual who is able to perform that service for you. You may be charged quite a large fee for that service, and to a certain degree, the quality of that attunement is affected by the nature, consciousness and energy of the attunor. On the positive side there exists the interaction between the one receiving and the one administering the attunement. There is the opportunity for feedback from each other and discussion of any experiences that may have occurred during the process.

If choosing to be attuned through the etheric, one must first be able to contact the etheric master, and be able to resonate at a frequency that is compatible to the attuning energy. These energies are much stronger and higher than those received from a physical attunement. During a physical attunement, the attuning energies are modified through the attunor, but only to the degree that that person can handle those energies herself.

To receive the following attunement etherically, first invoke your protection and whichever guides or Light beings you wish to be with. Then call for the master or the master of that ray, and ask if you may receive the attunement. If the answer is yes, sit in a meditative attitude and receive. When the attunement is completed you may ask the attuning master specifics as to the ray's use or any other questions you may have. Be sure to thank the master for the blessing just bestowed upon you.

It is important to recognize the moral responsibility one takes upon oneself when receiving these attunements. They are not something you saw one day, thought was cool, bought, and now you own to do with whatever you wish. They are gifts bestowed upon you. Whether you are consciously aware of it or not, each master who assists you establishes a permanent friendship and co-creative relationship with you. He/she is always there to support you, whether you give your conscious recognition or not. A loving bond is formed, and it is your responsibility to honor that bond and recognize it for the gift that it is. It is not to be flaunted to all your friends, but to be treated with reverence and dignity.

The following are the rays about which I have been asked to share information:

THE TRANSMUTATIONAL LIGHT BEAM

This beam comes directly from the Ashtar Command, a huge galactic assembly of angels, masters and various Light beings whose purpose is to assist Earth and her inhabitants during her transformation into a Light planet. We are all transmuting, but we may speed up that process by our conscious participation. Once you are joined to this beam it will remain with you, constantly working through the heavy energies within the cells of your bodies. If you should be working on a particular issue, you may ask for an extra dose of this ray to help transmute the energy of that issue. Ashtar tells me that this ray is for everyone and that they will adjust it to suit the vibration of the receiver. Many people who are working in their personal service through the guidance of the Ashtar Command have already been receiving this ray, the connection having been made on the inner planes. Ashtar explained to me that many Light workers have such strong, dark energies surrounding them, that the Command has not been able to penetrate these energies to form a working relationship. He asks that all who are drawn to this ray please make an effort to contact him, as the intention of contact will create an energetic space to permit anchoring of the light beam. The ray will then be joined to that person, transmuting the heavy energies and quickly advancing the spiritual growth and awareness of the receiver. Following is a brief comment from Ashtar regarding this ray.

"...Now let me explain the Transmutational Light Beam. This is a ray of energy sent from your intergalactic friends, which aids in the breaking away of those undesired energies that saturate the human cell. Those energies are slowly eaten away or transmuted, leaving room for more light to enter. This is the basis of the ascension process. We offer this light beam for all who would speed their transmutational process. We suggest this ray in use with all other healing modalities and especially with meditation, as meditation and petition to us will greatly increase the speed and depth of your transmuting. May you all receive the blessings you deserve. I AM Ashtar."

To be joined to this ray takes less than five minutes.

RAINBOW WARRIOR ATTUNEMENT

Channeled by Aleia O'Reilly from St. Germain and described in her book, *Rainbow Warriors Awake! An Invitation to Remember*, this is an ascension technique which assists in activating and building the Lightbody. Through a new vibrational color spectrum, the chakras are recalibrated, thereby activating the Lightbody of the "new human." Following are a few words I received from St. Germain on this process:

"The chakras of the Lightbody are being formed. This is done by realigning and recalibrating the seven known chakras. Using a different color spectrum than the original seven, a new chakra body is actually formed from the old. This then begins the development of an actual double body. Other processes are then performed as well on the Lightbody. So this calibration is only one aspect of forming that new vehicle for the human species. The attunement takes, as you know, anywhere from thirty to fifty minutes ... If the seven chakras are already cleaned and opened, much more good will come from this alignment. We will be able to create a much stronger body if we have greater functioning tools to work with ... The seven chakras are not just seven but many, and in truth we calibrate all of the major and minor chakras. For the most part the basic seven are worked with. This would depend on the individual and the level of healing already present in the body."

From this we can see that prior self-healing greatly facilitates the development of the Lightbody. Also, it would be good for all who desire this attunement to first activate their chakras, described under "Opening the Chakras." St. Germain told me that self-healing work and chakra opening done prior to this attunement will greatly facilitate the development of the Lightbody. The intensity of this attunement is often proportional to the size of the chakras.

There are other beings who assist him with the process, but he tells me that he, specifically, may be called on for the attunement. The Light beings who assist him will differ according to each individual receiver.

KWAN YIN ATTUNEMENT AND HEALING

Kwan Yin is considered the Goddess of Mercy and Compassion who hears the cries of the world and relieves suffering. She brings a healing, feminine, yin aspect which helps bring into harmony the imbalance of the male and female energies. She tells me most men would greatly benefit from her energies, and wishes that more would ask for her service. For women, she empowers the goddess energy within; especially to women who tend to be "girlish," imbalanced toward the yin side, she gives the goddess strength and power. As Kwan Yin performs the attunement, she may be seen moving about the body, realigning the yin and yang polarities. You may talk to her during the process. The attunement lasts approximately fifteen minutes and she tells me it is for everyone. She wishes all to be able to benefit from her energies.

KWAN YIN'S MAGNIFIED HEALING

Magnified Healing is the name given to a healing process channeled from Kwan Yin; this is a method utilizing certain colored healing energies channeled through the hands. It involves arm and hand motions representative of sacred geometry, the healing of self, others, and the Earth through various procedures, absentee healing, healing of karma, expansion of the three-fold flame of the heart, and a preparation for ascension technique. Kwan Yin states that she will personally be present each time Magnified Healing is used.

Magnified Healing is offered as a workshop. Upon completing the workshop one is qualified to teach the course. During the course an initiation to Kwan Yin and Magnified Healing is given, which is different from the Kwan Yin healing mentioned earlier.

REIKI I, II AND MASTER

Reiki is a powerful, multidimensional energy which, once attuned to, may be directed for healing on all levels of a person's being. This energy may be directed through the hands to a physical presence, or may be sent etherically. The possibilities and magnitude of Reiki are vast, though only a small portion of that energy is presently being utilized on the planet. The Reiki energy was once in common use but became lost over time. Mikao Usui rediscovered the ray in the early 1900's, making it available for our use today.

An individual is attuned to the Reiki energy gradually, over a period of three different sessions or workshops. Ordinarily the workshops follow the following format: In Reiki I the person receives his first Reiki attunement, begins the energy flowing through his hands and learns the basics of healing with Reiki. Reiki II teaches certain symbols to be used in conjunction with the Reiki energy. The symbols resonate a specific aspect of the Reiki ray, which assists in greater healing. Another attunement to even greater Reiki energy is given, along with practice of greater Reiki healing techniques. Reiki III or Reiki Master involves another Reiki attunement and learning the attunement process. At this point the person has mastered Reiki. In other words, that person has learned all the symbols and is able to attune others into Reiki, which qualifies her as a Reiki Master.

THE MASTER REIKI RAY

Those who have achieved Reiki Master have another ray available to them called the Master Reiki Ray. From the etheric, Dr. Usui provided this attunement to me and described it as a step up in energy from the Reiki Master attunement. This ray does not utilize symbols, as is common in Reiki, and works strictly with intention. Dr. Usui says that the recipient of this attunement must have received the first three levels, as these open the meridian, chakra and energy pathways through which the Reiki energy flows. All recipients to the Master Reiki Ray are at the discretion of Dr. Usui and need to contact him.

When using this ray in healing one need not direct it through the hands. For example, when doing self-healing, I do not need to lay my hands on my body for the energy to flow there. I simply ask that the Master Reiki Ray flow to, for example, my shoulders. The flow, in the form of massive amounts of energy, begins immediately. Then I ask for it to continue for as long as is appropriate. For distance healing, a technique taught in Reiki II, I direct the ray to my client without use of the customary symbols, nor do I need to direct it through my hands. Intention alone begins and sustains the flow.

When this attunement was performed on me, I saw myself as a Tibetan monk sitting on the floor of my room. I was in meditation and aware of sending out directed healing rays of energy. Then I stood up and walked through the courtyard. A dog walked passed me and as I touched his head, he immediately became energized. I noticed that whoever walked near me became rejuvenated. As I observed myself, I noticed a large crystalline energy that enveloped me. Next I saw the Master Jesus in his earthly incarnation as the Christ. I saw people walking by him and as they walked through his aura they were healed. The energy surrounding him appeared to be the same energy which I had seen around me. The energy extended from him and dispersed into the universe. This ray had a very loving essence and personality about it, which I recognized as a beloved friend whom I had not seen for a long time. I do not know what the ray was called at that time, but I recognize it today as the one we call Reiki. Dr. Usui said that I and others were friends and co-creators with this energy long ago. Those who walked with this energy then, are the ones to receive this Master Reiki Ray now. How much this ray affects a person depends on how clear he is when he receives it. The fewer dark energies being held within the bodies, the more room exists for the Reiki energy to anchor itself.

I have had some very profound experiences since receiving this ray. Without a doubt, it creates a spiritual resonance in those who come into contact with it. Immediately after receiving this ray, my clients' healing, even their life circumstances, began to skyrocket toward the positive. I have seen it over and over and have been astounded. Even associates of mine, with whom I was in close contact, began receiving markedly increased spiritual understandings. Realize that this has very little to do with me as a personality, other than my willingness and ability to carry large quantities of Light in the form of these various rays, and specifically the Master Reiki Ray.

The attunement is very gentle and takes about ten minutes. Understand that the preceding attunements and rays are not only for the benefit of the receiver. As Light workers, we are also Light carriers. As an example, picture the Earth and her atmosphere as dark grey. Within the grey is a latticework pattern of light surrounding the Earth. This latticework, which is actually her grid and ley lines, needs more light to sustain it. As more light is received, the latticework becomes larger and more intricate, becoming the planet's Lightbody. You might correlate this to your own meridian system and development of your own Lightbody. Now picture rays of brilliant Light coming towards the Earth, with the intention of anchoring into her center and strengthening her grids. As the Light hits her grey atmosphere, there is a clash — a repulsion — due to the vibrational disharmony of the two, yet a fraction of Light still manages to penetrate. Because of the darkness of the planet, the Light that penetrates needs help in anchoring itself, so it attaches to Light workers who are willing to carry it. Light workers will often gather at sacred sights or feel compelled to visit or move to certain locations which, unbeknownst to them, are situated on ley lines or vortexes, or in spiritually dark areas in need of their Light. Just by their presence, the Light that they carry anchors itself into the Earth at that particular spot. When one carries Light it also radiates to those who are around; others benefit as their own Light begins to grow simply by being within that presence. All of the preceding rays and attunements anchor more Light into the receiver. Everyone who chooses to receive these attunements benefits personally, and also provides a great service to others and to the planet herself. Think about it. Carrying Light is a wonderful thing!

UNDERSTANDING CONSCIOUSNESS

When one sees Eternity in things that pass away
and Infinity in finite things,
then one has pure knowledge.

— Bhagavad Gita

There is a significant difference between a third dimension warrior and a spiritual warrior. In the third dimension, a warrior is one who fights for a cause. The fight may be a physical one, such as in the crusades or the holy wars, or it may be passive fighting as typified by Martin Luther King, Jr. or the "passive resistance" of Mohandas K. Ghandi. The spiritual warrior, on the other hand, has no resistance. To the spiritual warrior, there is no "bad guy" — no opposition; no one that he needs to suppress. It is of paramount importance that the spiritual warrior understand the significance of all forms of intelligence and their co-creative purpose within the universe. Nothing opposes us. Not a destructive tornado, not a wild, dangerous animal, not a cancer cell. All play a role with us in the creation of the universe and in our personal realities. We who choose to live our lives for the purpose of removing darkness from ourselves, others, and the planet, and who choose to bring in Light, are spiritual warriors. Our "battle" is fought through co-creation and cooperation with all intelligences, be they of the Light or of the darkness.

First we must understand that Divine intelligence permeates the space within every atom and the space within the invisible (i.e. the air, ether, and the other dimensions). Then, from the very fact of its existence, we can deduce that as there is intelligence, there is purpose. What this purpose is, and how to communicate with it for the further fulfillment of the divine plan, is one of the intentions of this manual.

Let's look at something that is familiar to us. A dog, for example. In and of itself it is intelligent. It has the innate characteristic of "dog." I doubt whether anyone can honestly say that dogs do not serve some purpose on this planet. Now let's look a little deeper, at a dog's fur, for example. How does a cell know to become fur and not a toenail? And among dog fur, how does a poodle's fur know to grow curly instead of straight? This "knowing" what it is to be, and becoming that, is the intelligence within the cells.

So how great is that intelligence? That depends on your standard of measurement. To give a very simple example, can a fur cell teach law at a university? Obviously not. Can a lawyer be insulation, camouflage and protection for a dog? Obviously not. He can provide it for the dog, but he cannot "be" it himself. Both lawyer and cell have a purpose, and both possess the intelligence to fulfill that purpose. With purpose as the measure, neither is inferior to the other.

Where there is intelligence, there is the ability to communicate — the ability to exchange information through some means. We can communicate with hair. We can ask it to grow on a bald head, and if it chooses, it will oblige us and grow. However, having its own conscience and knowing its job of "hair" better than we do, it may refuse to grow, and if asked may state the reason. Perhaps there are conditions of the skin that do not permit hair growth. Perhaps there is a genetic pattern of baldness that the cell chooses to retain. Perhaps the individual, before incarnation, chose baldness for this life. The hair cell, knowing this, would not alter that plan.

All cells have within them the memory of their perfect form and function. When they reproduce, or replace themselves, they produce an identical replica of themselves. That's why you always look like you. Consider how often your skin cells slough off and how much hair you lose daily. If your cells did not have the intelligence to reproduce a replica of themselves, you might look like you today and someone else in a month!

Now let's look at something which we tend to see as the enemy, such as a cancer cell. Suppose this cell were once a healthy liver cell — one cell among thousands that collectively created a well-functioning human liver. But for some reason (and the reasons can be numerous), damage was done to this cell and it mutated. After mutation, it can no longer function as a healthy cell; it has become sick, you might say. Within its own intelligence it knows something is wrong and that it is not functioning properly. When the cell mutated, it produced a replica of its mutated self, all the while trying to function as a healthy liver cell. These mutated replicas produced more of themselves, creating cancer of the liver, or more correctly, hepatic cancer.

What about the cells that mutated? Are they evil? More importantly, are they out to get us? Are they our enemy, bound and determined to take over our bodies and render us a horrible death? Not at all. They have no more *intention* of harming, than fleas do as they infest a dog. The flea is simply acting on its innate instincts of survival through the ingestion of blood; the dog has merely become its home. Why then, one might ask, if the liver cells meant no harm, must we suffer the effects of their mutation?

First you must understand that we work with — co-create with — the entire universe. All forms of intelligence are interconnected at some level. To paraphrase an author (unfortunately, I cannot remember the author's name), "You cannot pick a flower, but you touch a star." Think about the significance of this. All consciousness stems from, and yet contains, the consciousness of the Divine Source. All consciousness is interconnected. We have cooperated with the consciousness of liver to create mutated liver cells. Why would we create something horrible for ourselves? Perhaps we have incurred a negative karma in this or another life, for which such an illness may clear us of our karmic debt. Perhaps we have had such disrespect for our body that we abused it beyond its limits of balance, and as a result, the cells broke down and disease stepped in. Perhaps we experience this now, so that in a future time we will have learned to honor our bodies and all intelligence within it. Actually, the reasons that one's higher Self may choose illness are numerous, and go beyond the scope of this manual.

Here's an analogy of this concept. Lets say you were given a job to do which you did very well, but one day you were feeling poorly and your performance was off. Your employer noticed that you weren't working up to par, and even made a comment about it. The next day you felt even worse than the day before, and your performance began to show marked decline. Now your employer is becoming seriously annoyed. You feel the pressure on you, but no matter how hard you try, your failing health takes its toll on your work. On top of that, you have the pressure of your illness and the pressure of an increasingly angry, relentless boss. How would that make you feel? The illness is bad enough, but a remorseless boss who didn't even bother to try to understand your situation, might eventually bring you to the end of your rope. You might quit your job, separate yourself from your employer, and wallow in your illness until (or if) you regain your health.

You, in the above example, represent the intelligence of a body that has become ill and is no longer able to function well (as in the cancerous liver cell). The unrelenting employer is the individual who is angry with his body for becoming ill. He sends negativity to his now dysfunctional cells, adding more strain to this already stressed consciousness. If the body receives no support, it will eventually go rampant in its frenzy to repair itself, and death from the illness may occur.

But what if he were to send love and understanding to that ailing consciousness? Doesn't love support you when you feel badly? Does understanding not help to speed your recovery much more than being criticized for being sick in the first place? Sending positive, sensitive feelings to an ailing body greatly helps to speed its recovery, and it helps in preventing illness in a healthy body.

What I am saying is that if we have a nurturing, communicative relationship with the consciousness within our bodies, we may be told exactly what is needed to heal that body. It may not be a drug at all, but rather a change of attitude, a vibrational remedy, or perhaps just a little healing energy sent that way. This is not to say that I am opposed to allopathic healing as I believe that all forms of healing have their place. Unfortunately, most drugs tend to relieve or suppress an ailment at the expense of another part of the body, and may alleviate the symptoms but fail to address, or cure, the cause. Therefore, if you could heal by cooperating, honoring and speaking to your body, wouldn't you rather do that than fill it full of potentially harmful chemicals? But, if allopathic medicine is taken, and there are definite times when this is appropriate (should I ever be laying on the road bleeding to death from a car accident, please don't let me continue to bleed while you only give me healing energy; get me to a hospital *and* give me healing energy!), speak to your body and ask it to accept the benefits of the drug, while rejecting the harmful effects.

What if you were to speak to your sore elbow, ask it to begin the healing process, and it refused? If your attitude tended toward indignation, remember that your elbow knows more about its function than you do. You must respect that it knows what it is doing. On some level, you may not be ready to release the pain, or you may not have learned the lesson that the pain offers. Whatever the case, you cannot go to war with a consciousness and try to force your wishes upon it. If you understand that at some time, on some level, you co-created the pain, then you can understand that you must also be a co-creator in healing the pain. The healing simply won't happen until all elements are ready for it to take place. If you should fuss and argue to have your way with this consciousness, you merely create a resistance and, as stated in the beginning of this chapter, spiritual warriors resist nothing. We honor and cooperate. We have full and total respect for all consciousness — never inflicting our will, always asking to work in unison.

In summary, we can say that everything within the universe has consciousness, and therefore intelligence. We are co-creators with all intelligence and are able to communicate with it. Our bodies are an example of this concept. We are composed of numerous intelligences, from our organs to the consciousness of each individual cell, and when honored and acknowledged, the chance of illness decreases. Using this process of communication, illness itself can be healed on the very deepest levels, permitting a complete cellular resolution of the dysfunction.

The remainder of Part II is dedicated to listing, with brief descriptions, the intelligences that we may encounter. A deeper explanation of their function and personalities is included in Part III under the descriptions of the corresponding release techniques. These intelligent energies are invisible to the third-dimensional eye, but this in no way negates their existence nor their effect upon us. Many of these energies are harmful to our spiritual and physical growth, so as spiritual warriors, the better we understand them, the more capable we are of freeing ourselves and others from their negative effects.

DESCRIPTIONS OF VARIOUS FORMS OF INTELLIGENCE

The astral plane is known to have seven dimensions. The most debauched forms of intelligence exist in the first dimension, increasing in spiritual consciousness up to the seventh, which may be considered a form of heaven. Level seven may be considered a form of heaven. There are other planes and dimensions beyond the astral level, but for our purpose we will focus on the lower astral region where many unpleasant energies exist.

The forms of intelligence that dwell within the lower astral plane range from interesting at best, to horrifying. If a person were to create "hell" for himself after death, it would exist in this region. Within this plane dwell all kinds of undesirable intelligences that may attach to people's energy fields as parasitic, energy-draining vampires. These nasties may remain attached to a person through several incarnations. Many of these attachments occurred through curses, spells, or even simply from harmful thoughts cast upon the victim. It's also possible that the individual was exposed to, or participated in, the black arts during a present or past life experience. What to do with these nasties is explained in Part III.

The most common types of these energies are:

CREATURES

Creatures range from various kinds of insects to snakes and other reptiles. They may be found living in the astral body of a person, draining his energy. Their attitude is one of survival, and their host's energy field is where they choose to live. They have no sense of justice or right or wrong. They merely exist.

NEGATIVE THOUGHT FORMS AND THOUGHT FORM MONSTERS

There is no exaggeration in the expression "What we think, we create." Continual mental energy exerted towards an idea will eventually bring that idea to life. Literally. Such a life is called a "thought form." We will not concern our-selves with the positive thought forms, as we like having them around; however, the negative ones can give us a world of trouble. For example, a parent may have the thought about his child, "You'll never be any good." Over the years, the thought grows into a living energy that is directed at the child and becomes attached to the child's energy field. As the child grows to become an adult, he believes and therefore creates a life supporting the concept of being no good, as the thought form, now being part of his energy, has become part of him. Clairvoyantly seen, this thought form hangs in the energy field like a black or grey cloud.

The process of creating a thought form can be taken a step further, in which the thinker "thinks" a monster. The thought form thus created takes on the actu-al form of the monster, as opposed to being just a cloud of energy. These are usu-ally created to dwell within and torment people. The monsters look like the cre-ator's concept of a monster, and are given the creator's intention for his use. They may be created specifically to torture the astral form of a particular person. These types of thought forms, which look like monsters and are very difficult to distin-guish from Dark Forces, can be seen attached to an individual's energy field, or just lurking around in the astral plane.

ASTRAL MONSTER PROJECTILES

Very similar to thought form monsters are astral monster projectiles. With the astral monster a thought form monster is first created, but rather than being formed only from thought, the monster's creator projects his own astral matter, from his astral body, into the form of his intended creation. The monster is then directed to a target with the purpose of bringing harm.

Because the monster takes life from the creator's own energy field, it is actu-ally a projectile of the creator and can be reabsorbed back into the creator's astral body, thus ending the projectile's existence. Dark Forces use this same technique, as one Dark Force can have hundreds of projectiles attached to unknowing indi-viduals, places or things.

IMPLANTS

Implants tend to be receptors, transmitters, or monitoring devices. These are usually found associated with extraterrestrial activity and are often attached to the astral or etheric body of the host. I mention them here because they are inva-sive, frequently cause physical pain and can be a hindrance to spiritual growth. I might add that most, but not all, implants are harmful. As more Light workers awaken and step into their service, the Galactic Federation has made available what we might loosely call "transmutational implants." These implants are used to accelerate the cellular healing process by increasing the vibratory rate of the cells. This is a very general explanation and they, in fact, do much more than I have mentioned. Merely be aware that there are negative and positive implants, though most that you will encounter will be of the negative sort.

DEVICES

Like implants, devices are most often found both within the etheric and astral bodies of the host. The most common are seen as protective cages or bands placed around the heart. Such devices could have been created by the individual in this or a past life, or they could have been put there by a medicine man or witch doctor. Knives and swords are also frequently seen along with accompanying rips and tears in the astral body.

MIND/SOUL FRAGMENTS OR "SOUL RETRIEVAL"

A mind/soul fragment is similar to, but not to be confused with, an out-of-the-body experience. In fragmentation, a part of the individual's consciousness leaves the body. It is still connected by the silver cord, so it can be reintegrated, but it does not have the ability to reintegrate on its own as it is not aware that is has become separated. The fragment, (the portion of the consciousness that split) may have occurred in this lifetime or it may have fragmented lifetimes ago and actually be residing on another planet. It may float behind the individual like a balloon on a string, or it may have attached to another person. Fragmentation usually occurs during severe trauma, frequently during childhood. A part of the victim's consciousness couldn't bear a certain pain anymore, went off into some fantasy or place of emotional safety, and didn't come back. Fragments can be spoken to and generally retain the age and memory from the time of their fragmentation, but have no memory beyond that. Though mind/soul fragments are not intentionally negative, they can attach to another person and will have the same effect as an attached discarnate being. They also leave the fragmented person incomplete, as the person is literally "not all there."

EXTRATERRESTRIALS

There are many extraterrestrials, physical and discarnate, on the planet at this time. Some intend us harm, some provide assistance, and some are simply observers. This book is primarily concerned with those who attach to a person's energy field and cause harm. These are beings who bypass the incarnation process and experience earth life through the astral body of a human. They attach to the human's energy field and have the same effect as a discarnate entity attachment. Unlike discarnate attachments, however, attached extraterrestrials usually know what they're doing and are often just curious. Some mean no harm, while others are so totally possessed by Dark Forces that they are to be treated in a similar manner as the dark angels. The way in which we respond to them depends on their intention. Unless they are parasitic in someone's energy field or have dark intentions, if they don't bother us, we needn't bother them.

In Part III, I do not include a section for releasing extraterrestrials because there is no particular method used on them. You must determine whether their intention is to cause harm or not. If they are within someone's energy field but mean no harm, release them as you would a discarnate, described under the chapter, "Release of Earthbound Discarnates." If they are definitely of the dark, release as you would a Dark Force, described under, "Release of Dark Forces."

DISCARNATE EARTHBOUND ENTITIES OR "GHOSTS"

The death experience is such that a person exits his physical body through severance of the silver cord. Waiting to greet him are either angelic beings or deceased loved ones who stand within a field of Light. This Light is believed to be somewhere within the middle astral plane. From there, the deceased goes to one of the seven planes within the astral dimension that vibrates best with his level of consciousness. A very low consciousness would go to one of the lower regions with like-minded people, whereas a person with a very high spiritual vibration would enter one of the higher astral planes. The newly discarnate being lives within his astral body until it eventually wears away, after which he incarnates and starts the process again. This cycle continues until he has spiritually progressed to the point of no longer needing to experience physical life.

Ideally, this is how the process works. Unfortunately, it doesn't always turn out this way. The Light is always there at a person's death, but for numerous reasons, a person might not enter it but choose to reside within his astral or etheric body on the earth plane. This now discarnate being may wander the earth until his astral body wears away, or until he is rescued. The sad affair with such an earthbound soul is that he is literally in a type of purgatory. As he has not entered the Light after death, he has no more knowledge regarding his situation than he did when he was alive. In other words, he is not one bit more enlightened or spiritually aware than he was while still in his physical body. Earthbound souls are always tremendously confused, not believing themselves to be in either heaven or hell, and frequently not even believing themselves to be dead. To them, their existence is a living nightmare. I have known earthbound souls to be in this condition for over one hundred years. In the astral plane there is no sense of linear time, as we know it, so one hundred years does not appear as long to them as it would to us. However, it does take its toll emotionally.

The plight of the discarnate, or earthbound soul, is often a very difficult thing for incarnate people to understand. We tend to think, "How could a person not know that he is dead?" One reason for this is that we imagine so much drama accompanying the death process. We think "something happens" when a person dies. Understand that consciousness is ever-existing. There is no "something happens" to consciousness. In cases of sudden death, as might occur in a car accident or from a fatal acute heart attack, the person has no awareness of impending death, therefore no time to prepare his consciousness for it.

For example, one minute a man may be standing in the kitchen, and the next minute he's standing outside his body, looking at his physical body lying on the kitchen floor. The last thing he remembered was feeling ill and falling down. He's wondering how it could be that he's looking at his body, when he knows perfectly well that his body is with him. (He observes his etheric and astral bodies which appear physical to him.) He runs to get his wife, terrified because something horrible has happened, but he doesn't understand what. He yells for her attention, but she can't hear him. He reaches to shake her, but his hand penetrates her body. In his terror and confusion, he is now caught in a living nightmare. Eventually his wife will find his physical body, and, as the invisible observer, he will follow his body to the morgue and attend his own funeral. Then, with nowhere to go and nothing to do, he may hang around his house and his wife, possibly being seen at times and therefore referred to as a "ghost." He also has another option, which is our main concern in this manual. He may go to his wife and "join" her by merging with her astral matter. In this condition he is able to experience the sensations of the physical body through her. However, as he is now sharing her energy field and not living entirely within his own, he has become a parasite, constantly draining her of her energy and strength. Not only that, but whatever illness he has, he brings with him, which may manifest in her physical body. For example, if he had arthritis of the knees, she may notice her knees beginning to ache. He may also influence her, through her subconscious mind, with his thoughts and desires. If he drank alcohol, but she didn't, he may begin to project his desire for alcohol onto her. As she receives that desire through her subconscious, she interprets it as simply wanting a drink. Because they now share the same energy field, she cannot distinguish this desire as being other than her own, may follow up on it and begin drinking. When she dies and goes into the Light, he may either go with her, or, as he knows her body is dying, he may disconnect and find another body with which to merge.

I want to make it perfectly clear that I am not implying that all sudden death victims become earthbound. The above illustration is merely an example of the dynamics that may lead to this type of condition.

The existence of an earthbound discarnate is grim, at best. I've attempted as briefly and simply as possible, to define and give a little information so that you may better understand the condition. I do not feel that you need much detail as to the why's and wherefore's of these beings. A tome could be written on it. What is important is to have a sense of empathy. Understand their condition, and it will be much easier to release them.

One would think that discarnate beings would be excited to be educated and directed to the Light. This is usually not the case. Losing their physical bodies was trauma enough. After they adjust to that situation, rarely are they ready to go through what they might consider another trauma. After all, if they understood the concept of a positive spiritual existence after death, they need merely think of that experience and it would occur for them. The fact that they have not considered this, holds them in their purgatory. Consequently, when given the offer to be released to the Light, why should they believe it? Here, again, we must return to honoring consciousness. These discarnates have as much right *not* to enter the Light as we have to suggest it to them. It is their free will. If you understand how they feel and show them some compassion, it will be much easier to release them. By the way, the makers of the movie "Ghost" did a wonderful job of depicting the plight of an earthbound discarnate. Though the movie may appear fanciful and "Hollywood," it is surprisingly accurate. I recommend it.

ANGELS, DARK AND LIGHT

There is one more type of being with whom we will concern ourselves — the angels.

THE DARK ANGELS

The most feared, misunderstood and horrible beings within our planetary system are the Dark Forces, sometimes referred to as "devils" or "demons." As to their origin, the myths abound. We do know that they are of the angelic realm. As I understand and have come to believe, the angel of Light, Lucifer, took part of his essence, removed all Light, and thereby created a dark version of himself. This dark version, named Satan, was directed to the earth and its surrounding dimensions, taking one-third of the angelic realm with him for the purpose of bringing duality to this planet. Their only purpose is destruction. They were not a mistake, as taught in certain religions. There was no, "Oops! Somehow we got these bad guys. What do we do, now?" No, they were planned, and as is true of all other creations, they have a purpose with which we are co-creators.

Let's consider what our planet is about. Why do humans reside here? Why have we chosen to come to *this* planet with its sickness and pain? Why didn't we pick a place void of duality, without black and white, good and bad, life and death? We chose this because it offered what we needed for our soul's growth. We needed to experience duality. We *wanted* to experience duality! Earth is not a prison; we weren't condemned to be here. Someone or something has to create the duality for us to experience, which is the purpose of the Dark Forces. When we come to earth, they are simply part of the package. The more we want to learn or experience, the more they exert their influence over us. At birth, each one of us is endowed with a certain number of these dark energies. Throughout our lives, we may lose some, or we may acquire more, depending on our lifestyle and consciousness. When such a time comes that we think and live in a divine space, then we have grown beyond the power of the dark ones. Remember, in the history of our being, we have not always been Light workers. There was a time when we were under a strong pull of darkness. By our will, we have grown beyond this influence. However, as far as I know, none of us are yet perfect, so until the dark ones no longer serve us, and have been removed, we have their attachments in our fields.

What about the concept of possession — the situation in which Dark Forces totally take over an individual. Is it real? Does it happen? Yes to both. Possession can be in any or all of the bodies. If physical, the person may be racked with pain and disease. If emotional or mental, the person may be insane or a psychopathic murderer. I believe most people in mental institutions would have at least a seventy-five percent cure rate if their Dark Forces were removed. I also maintain that the veterans hospitals would not be nearly as crowded if war veterans were depossessed of their innumerable discarnate attachments and Dark Forces. There is no place like a war zone to bring out the most ghastly of dark energies, or to abound with the discarnate souls of sudden death victims.

Every adult you meet has Dark Force and discarnate attachments — some more than others — unless the attachments have been removed. If we associate among the lower vibrations, we are obviously on their turf. Drugs, bars, drunkenness and prostitution are the most common haunts and situations that attract these types of energies. People who dabble in such areas are frequently "drawn into" them, and then have a very difficult time getting out. One reason is that their attachments have become so strong, through association in such places, that the subconscious influence of these attachments overwhelms their own better judgment or will power. In the case of the ordinary person, or even one consciously striving toward spiritual growth, the number of attachments still depends on his history, regardless of his present spiritual striving. As one raises one's consciousness and vibrations through spiritual intentions and practices, one's earthbound attachments may be open to this growth, benefit from it, and thereby create a situation for their own rescue. This would not be the case with attached Dark Forces, however. These dark angels' purpose is to hold all things in darkness, so they have no intention of anyone growing spiritually. In fact, they often attack those who hinder their work. For this reason, Light workers are frequent targets for the Dark Forces.

Suppose a person chooses the spiritual path. How is he then affected by his Dark Force attachments? If he has yet to learn a particular soul lesson that would be learned through the influence of such an attachment, that attachment will either not release during a releasement session, or it will release, but be replaced by another. On the other hand, because consciousness is raising so quickly and the molecular structure of Earth and everything on her, including us, is speeding up, many people are beyond the need of some or all of their Dark Force atttachments, therefore they no longer serve a purpose and are ready to be released. It is these individuals who are best served in releasement work.

For those who think, "I don't believe in the Dark Forces, therefore they can't hurt me," permit me to shatter an illusion. Denial of the dark ones increases their power. How much easier is it to influence someone if that person believes his ideas are his own? How much easier is it to control without resistance? Denial of the Dark Forces puts one right into their hands.

Another illusion is to think, "I meditate. I'm on a spiritual path. I resonate too highly for them to affect me." Wrong again. The dark angels are very power-ful within their energy field and can tolerate a great amount of Light. They can even transform themselves to appear as angels of Light to dupe their victims. However, they cannot tolerate this masquerade very long, and will eventually have to return to their darkened state. There are very few incarnate humans whose auras are so pure and who resonate so highly, that a Dark Force cannot live within them. I personally would not suggest permitting one's self the luxury of that particular illusion. When one has become spiritually well-integrated, how-ever, and has reached a high level of mastery and initiation (discussed under the "Ascension/Transmutation" chapter), she is surely beyond any need for further attachment. Until then, a powerful, spiritually magnetized aura, plus the protec-tion of the angels of Light, will protect one from further attachment, once these entities have been released.

The point I want to make clear is that everyone has Dark Force attachments; they are part of the human package. Over lifetimes, as we grow spiritually, our consciousness raises beyond the level of their influence. In each lifetime, if we continue to grow, we will incarnate with fewer Dark Forces than the previous life. Soon, in this particular cycle of Earth's history, Dark Forces will no longer be per-mitted. What we are doing now is assisting in that process by releasing them from ourselves and the Earth. Therefore many people are ready to have their Dark Forces removed, as they no longer serve any purpose for their growth. Soon they will be released from the entire planet.

Dark Forces attach not only to people, but to plants and animals as well. For example, they may dwell in forests. If you've ever been in a forest that gives you "the creeps," you may be feeling the effects of an astral war being enacted on that site, with its accompanying Dark Forces. They are also known to dwell within the earth and infest land in general.

For further understanding of these beings, I suggest reading *Dark Robes, Dark Brothers* by Hilarion. I also suggest reading excerpts from two books by the Master Djwhal Khul, channeled through Alice Bailey. One is the book *Ponder on This* (see page 62, under "Dark Forces"). The other is *Serving Humanity* (see page 496, under "Dark Forces"). William Baldwin's book, *Spirit Releasement Therapy*, is also highly recommended. (See Recommended Readings.)

THE LIGHT ANGELS

When our consciousness withdraws from our third-dimensional, conscious, waking state and wanders into the astral world, we are meandering in realms in which we are not overly empowered. In the lower astral realms, where we will do some of our release work, there are any number of "uglies" that may confront us, or dark beings lurking around the corner, waiting for a chance to pounce. As these realms are strange turf to us, the universe has kindly provided escorts and bodyguards in the form of angels of Light. Not only do these angels take an active part in assisting us with the release of dark beings and energies (described in detail in Part III), but they also lend us protection through various means. During interdimensional work they can be seen observing and standing by — ready to help us along when we're not sure of our next step. They literally escort us and stand guard around us, holding back any darkness that may interfere. Remember, as spiritual warriors, we co-create with all consciousness. Without the co-creative help of the angels of Light, we would not be able to release or rescue any of the previously mentioned entities. We need their help. We work together. We're a team of spiritual warriors.

Our greatest allies in our releasement work with the Dark Forces are Archangel Michael and his spiritual warrior band of angels. Archangel Michael and his angels have specifically chosen, as their service and with our help, to remove illusion and darkness from this planet. Before any entity removal work is begun, consider establishing a relationship with this mighty angel. With your intention or focused concentration, call him to you and carry on a friendly conversation. Tell him your intentions to work interdimensionally and ask him to assist you. Speaking to him ahead of time may give you a greater sense of security. Even if you don't do this and you have serious intentions of doing interdimensional work (if this is part of your service in this lifetime), then rest assured that the relationship has already been established on a spiritual plane. It is then only for you to instigate the relationship on a conscious level. Also there to help us are the ascended masters, who are not of the angelic realm, in addition to any number of very evolved beings.

Anyone doing interdimensional work should be able to concentrate in an altered state, see or sense with the inner eye, and have some form of communication with his spiritual guidance. It is then merely a matter of directing one's intentions toward Archangel Michael, stating one's desire to clean up the astral and physical planes of dark intelligences, dark energies, and earthbound discarnates, and then asking for his assistance.

I have explained the major dark energies that hinder the bringing in of Light. The releasing techniques for these energies now follow.

PART III

THE TECHNIQUE

Whatever you can truly convince the mind you can do, you can do.
Since everything is made out of mind, it can be controlled by mind.
As you develop more and more mental strength,
ultimately you will be able to do anything.

— Paramahansa Yogananda, *The Divine Romance*

I have written these instructions in a healer-to-client format, as I feel it may be easier to practice on another rather than on oneself. You may discover that in the beginning you might be more objective concerning your vision and insights when applied to someone else. Also, with two people involved, a feedback loop is created, whereas by yourself you may wonder, "Did I really see it?" and "Is it really gone?" The reader may incorporate all of the following techniques, or utilize only those which fit best within his own personal system, therefore the techniques are separated into sections for ease of use. Also note that the pronouns he/she and him/her have been used randomly and without any intention of gender bias.

I am not a medical doctor, and unless you are, we are not treating, prescribing or practicing medicine, so a thorough medical knowledge is not necessary for this type of work. However, when scanning the body while doing Cellular Memory Release, it is very helpful to know what organ you are seeing. Therefore I have included some simple anatomy diagrams. For more information on anatomy and for some basic explanations of the functions of certain organs, I suggest *The Anatomy Coloring Book*, by Wynn Kapit and Lawrence Elson.

After having undergone Cellular Memory or attachment release sessions, the client should drink several glasses of pure water a day for several days. This will assist the cells in flushing out the released energies. She must also soak in one to two cups of sea salt to a full tub of water for at least twenty minutes on the day of the release. This will help pull any residual released energies out from the aura, and soothe the aura. If sea salt is not available, one cup of Epsom salt may be substituted.

Be aware that energies release in layers. We've built up our "stuff" over lifetimes, and what we are trying to do now is to release it all in one. Therefore, even though instantaneous healings may occur in certain areas, other areas of dysfunction will improve more gradually over time.

PROTECTION

Angels and ministers of grace, defend us!

— William Shakespeare, *Hamlet*

Whenever we go into an altered state or take our awareness to other dimensions, we leave ourselves somewhat vulnerable to negative energies. For this reason, a meditation for protection is a prerequisite. There are many forms of self-protection, and although I do not presume to know what is best for you, there are certain techniques I can suggest:

1. When surrounding yourself with Light, a mixture of gold, white and silver is stronger than either by itself. After creating the Light, anchor it around you, intending for it to remain throughout your session. I personally call the white ray, silver ray and gold ray. When I feel their presence, I ask them to shower their Light upon me. I feel the energy go through me and into my auric field. I repeat this three times, expanding the Light further out in my field. I ask that the Light strengthen my aura and be impenetrable to anything but my highest good. I anchor the Light there and thank the angels. Understand that white Light is unconditionally loving and does not desire to change whatever comes into its presence. Rather, it accepts all energies. For that reason, white Light alone is not the priority choice for protection. For instance, the Dark Forces can change themselves into white beings to deceive an observer, even though they cannot hold the white vibration very long. Since the white Light is unconditionally loving and non-discerning, it can actually give energy to the dark beings who know how to manipulate it for their own purposes. It is excellent, however, for healing and for raising one's own vibrations. It also helps keep the less sophisticated negative energies (such as other people's thoughts and emotions) from penetrating one's energy field.

Gold, silver and purple light are also excellent for protection and for sending to others, as these colors, especially the gold and purple are conditional — they tend to draw one toward the heart.

2. Visualize yourself sitting in the middle of a huge violet flame. The flame is around and through you. This is St. Germain's violet transmuting flame. It will transmute polluted energies that may come into your field while you are doing interdimensional work. Remember that all energies are connected, so even if you are doing a remote release session on someone, you may easily become contaminated by their energies, just as if you were physically working in their energy field. It is therefore advisable to sit within the flame and ask that it remain around you during your entire session.

3. Invoke whichever spiritual guidance you work with, as well as the guidance of your client. Archangel Raphael and his angels work frequently with healing and may be invoked. During discarnate release work, the Dark Forces will often try to interfere. It is here that you want to call Archangel Michael and his angels; ask them to guard you and hold back all darkness that might interfere.

4. Other protection that may be used is to visualize a flaming blue cross which will resonate at a high level of energy. You can anchor this cross near you, or bring it down, lying horizontal, into your house or office. You can bring one cross down from the ceiling and one up from the ground.

5. Whenever you are releasing Dark Forces and discarnates, ask for, and sense, Archangel Michael's flaming blue sword suspended between you and the client. I have had these beings fling themselves at me in anger, but they were immediately repelled upon contacting the sword.

Whenever you do any protection techniques, don't go on until you see, or sense, that they are accomplished. In other words, once you have asked the angels to stand around you, don't continue until you have some sense of their presence. In any healing work, you may well have periods of doubt, but knowing (through sense or sight) that the angels are there to assist often helps build self confidence.

CELLULAR MEMORY RELEASE

He who sees the Lord within every creature,
Deathlessly dwelling amidst the mortal,
That man sees truly.

— Bhagavad Gita

Cellular Memory Release is a technique that releases past memory of pain from the cells through educating the body consciousness. Over lifetimes a human's body collects pain in the form of memory within the cells. In this lifetime, when our physical or emotional "stuff" comes up, it is merely a conscious manifestation of stored memory. Light workers are presently in a period in which their earthly third-dimensional incarnations are coming to an end. This is so because the Earth and humans are "ascending" to a higher form in which death and pain as we presently know them, will no longer be a reality. The new human species will no longer dwell in a material, physical form, but rather in a body of Light, sometimes referred to as the Lightbody, which will be void of the dark energies that the human physical form presently carries. The ascension will occur over a period of time and should be completed within the next seventeen years, which is within most of your lifetimes. What this means is that death, pain and disease are no longer a necessary reality for most of you. I say "most" and not "all" because some Light workers have chosen to work on the physical plane for a while, leave their body by way of death, and then continue to work from the other side. But for most of us, death as we know it, is no longer inevitable.

In Cellular Memory Release we educate the body consciousness that it is now time to live, not die — to rejuvenate, not deteriorate — that it no longer needs to hold pain and dysfunction as a learning tool for us, but rather, for the most part, we have learned those lessons. Therefore, the benefit that the bodies have rendered us by holding those memories no longer serves us. Rather, they can better serve us by permitting us to grow spiritually and evolve into Light beings. To accomplish this we need the bodies to release stored memory of pain, both emotional and physical, thus clearing the cells of dark energies. After being cleared, the cells can hold more Light, resonate higher and assist in building a Light body.

This is one of the most powerful techniques a person can use for her personal healing. Once the body consciousness understands that it is finally time to heal and that all the pain it has endured may terminate in this lifetime, it goes for it! The healing takes place, not only in the body, but the circumstances surrounding the individual begin to change also, all towards the person's spiritual benefit. I am constantly amazed at how my client's lives change after their bodies agree that now is the time to heal. This is the lifetime they have been waiting for!

Then again, not everyone is ready to release all their pain and issues. This is why one should never become attached to the outcome of one's session. A person may heal tremendously on numerous levels, but one particular pain or issue may appear to remain unresolved. This is almost always the case when that person has not yet learned, or grown, from the issue the pain represents. This is also the case when releasing Dark Forces; some may return because the client has not yet fully benefited from their influence. When the issue has been resolved, then the dark energies release and the healing takes place.

This releasement is targeting very, very deep emotions and memories of traumas from the entirety of a person's existence. With the nature of this work, the client may, but does not have to remember the traumas being released. For the most part, all the client experiences is a diffuse "something" leaving and a feeling of lightness and calm after the session. If a conscious physical pain is being released, it is often felt immediately. For example, I remember an abscessed tooth of a former client. I had asked the nerves in her tooth to begin healing, and explained that this infection no longer served a purpose. As the tooth was healing, there remained a persistent ache, which she asked me to remove. I joined with the tooth's consciousness and asked the pain to release. It was instantly gone, the whole process taking no more than four minutes. I cannot guarantee that pain will always leave this quickly using this technique, but it has worked for me more times than not.

When first speaking to a particular body consciousness, understand that this consciousness has had many lifetimes of doing its own thing, without ever having been acknowledged, spoken to, or honored. This will be a new experience for it, and what you present will also be new. This intelligence has the right not to follow your wishes, but given more information as to the reasoning behind your wishes, it may oblige.

To call upon the body consciousness of a client, go into an undisturbed space, do your protection, and invoke your guidance. Then call, up to three times, the name of your client. Wait until you see or sense her before you. If this is a person you have never met or seen, call the name on her birth certificate and state her birthday. You also might ask her height, weight and hair color and length before you do the session. This way, with her birthday, you're sure to get the right Sue Smith, and not one of the many Sue Smiths on the planet. If you do a session on a client while they are on the phone with you, you can simply tune into their energy as you speak to them. I rarely do sessions over the phone, however. In my experience, the anxiety over long-distance telephone charges is distracting. Not only must they pay me, but if out of town, they pay for a long distance call while waiting for me to finish.

I establish a time when I am going to do the session remotely and the time that they will call me back to discuss the results. This way they can go into a meditative state and experience it if they choose, or they can go about their daily routine and not take time out. Whether the client is tuned in or oblivious during the session is unimportant; the effect will be the same.

When you have the client before you, join with her body consciousness. This is the consciousness that regulates the functions of the bodies — you might consider it the oversoul of the bodies. You can join with the body consciousness with your intention, but I find I have a much better reception if I ask the consciousness to join with me. I do this every time I want a two-way conversation with any intelligence.

Let's pretend that I'm working on "John." I use the client's name frequently when speaking to the body consciousness, for the purpose of emphasis. You need not parrot my words, but some words and phrases seem to really "get it" better than others. I will give you the gist of what to say and then how I say it.

"I speak directly and specifically with the body consciousness of John. I ask John's body consciousness to join with my consciousness, now."

When it joins with me, which is immediate, I feel the joining as a slight jolt on my aura. You may perceive it in some other way, or simply sense that it is with you. I then honor the consciousness and explain why I am there. Often the consciousness responds back and a dialogue ensues. A sample conversation might be as follows.

"I thank you for all that you are and all that you've done for John. All pain, grief and dysfunction held within the cells of these bodies have been a service to John and helped in his growth. But things are changing, now. The planet is going through a change to a higher consciousness, and all those upon the planet must raise in consciousness also, if

they wish to remain here. There is no longer room for heavy or negative energies. John is ready to consciously embody his divine essence and build his Lightbody. He can't do this while these energies of pain and dysfunction hold him back. The time has come for these heavy energies to transmute to a higher consciousness, as they no longer serve a purpose. I ask that these energies be of service to John by speeding up their own evolution and transmuting to a higher vibration. So I ask that all pain and anything less than divine perfection, which dwells within the DNA and within all bodies, leave now."

At this point the consciousness may wish to discuss what you have just presented; take time to listen. You may perceive a mist or fog rise from your client as the energies release. See this either go into a violet flame or white/gold Light, and intend it to be transmuted.

Even though you have already explained your intentions to the body consciousness, you will explain it many more times to the individual aspects of consciousness within the body before the session is over. Each one has its own function, and will not be so ready to change just because you ask it to. Considerable diplomacy is frequently required. Remember, an energy will not release, nor a dysfunction correct itself if it still serves the client. This is not something you will necessarily know. If an energy refuses to leave, or only releases a little, understand that this intelligence knows more about its purpose than you do. Never argue or create a resistance! Accept that everything you do must work within the divine plan, and that you don't always know what that plan is.

Next, scan the internal body. You may see the physical as well as the etheric, or only the physical, or you may see neither, but merely "know." Personally, what I see is the etheric organ, or matter. I may see an enlarged heart, when the actual physical heart is of normal size. This means a problem of enlargement has occurred in the etheric heart, which, if not treated, will manifest in the physical. Or, I may see an enlarged etheric heart, only to find that the client had been diagnosed as having an enlarged physical heart by a medical doctor. Whichever the case, solving the dysfunction would be the same: By asking the pain and grief to release, the factors which caused the enlargement will release, and subsequently, the enlargement will decrease or not proceed to manifest physically.

When scanning the body, I usually begin with the pituitary gland, which often resembles a prune. This consciousness can hold considerable anger and pain, and may not want to release at first. With all consciousness, the process is basically the same: Honor it first for all that it is, and all that it has done. State that the earth is raising its level of consciousness and vibration, and that pain and suffering will no longer be allowed. This person must release himself of these heavy energies so that he can be of greater service to the earth and better develop his Lightbody. The purpose served by holding this pain is no longer valid. Ask the intelligence to raise its own consciousness and speed its own spiritual evolution by releasing these energies. This, then, is its service to the client, and thereby its service to the planet.

From the pituitary I go to the pineal gland (which looks like a seed) and then to the eyes. The eyes are one of the most sorrowful intelligences in the body. They are full of pain and grief from all they have seen over so many lifetimes. Be prepared for the overwhelming emotions of sadness and anger that these various intelligences may hold.

Next comes the thymus gland which, like the pituitary, tends to atrophy in the adult, but when fully active it holds a very important role. Within the newly-transmuted human form, the thymus will again become fully functioning and will have its own corresponding chakra. Activating the thymus chakra is explained in the chapter "Opening the Chakras."

"I ask the thymus to release all pain, dysfunction, and anything less than divine perfection from the DNA and from all bodies, now. I ask the thymus to become fully active and remember its perfect form and function, now."

The eighth atom holds the holographic blueprint of an individual's makeup and distributes its information throughout the cells of the bodies as they are being developed. After the thymus, I usually address the eighth atom, asking it to release as described.

The areas I've described thus far are the ones I always approach in each cellular memory release session. After the eighth atom, I am guided where to go next. If I do not sense an organ specifically call to me, I continue to scan the body. I release anything that looks diseased or gives the impression that something is wrong. There is no part of our anatomy that has not stored some measure of grief. Everything from our skin to our toenails is in need of release.

During the first session of Cellular Memory Release, a client's individual intelligences tend to release very conservatively. One reason for this is that the intelligences are uncertain whether they want to do this, and another is that a person can only release so much before entering a healing crisis. The intelligences may also state that the client does not want to release. If the client is physically present, have him explain to the intelligence his feelings and intentions for healing. If he really is ready to release, he will. If he is not, but says that he is, the intelligence will know this and will not release anyway. If the session is being done remotely, call the client's higher Self and have it talk to the reluctant consciousness.

After the body consciousness has become used to the idea of releasing, asking it to do so becomes very simple. Rarely will you need to give a full explanation again. Simply say something like,

"I speak specifically to my gall bladder (for example) and ask that it release all pain, dysfunction, and anything less then divine perfection, from all bodies, and from the DNA now."

There are some intelligences which, as a general rule, are reluctant to release. They are the pituitary, the liver and the heart. The pituitary tends to hold considerable anger and is often defiant. With it, gentleness and reason work the best. The liver is reticent to release because it filters. It seems to believe that if it releases what it filters, it may do harm to the body, and that it should store and hold more than release. To the liver, state that it is time it had a bath, and that it would function much better if it released its energy of pain. Asking the liver to release does not necessarily mean that it will release toxins, but rather the negative energies which hold toxins bound within it. When enough of the energies are released, the toxins may then dump into the system. Dumping toxins seems to be the liver's concern and the reason why it is cautious about releasing. Note, however, that some people strive towards physical detoxifying and cleansing, at which time releasing the liver would be most appropriate. However, if the client is not consciously detoxifying, he may undergo a healing crisis if his liver should release an exorbitant amount of energy and toxins into his system. What I suggest is for you to use your common sense and trust that the liver knows what it's doing. Remember, never force your wishes on anything.

The heart is not to be confused with the heart chakra. The heart chakra takes in the higher energies of love and joy. The physical heart, however, is frequently smothered in feelings of pain, sorrow and anger, with etheric walls, chains, and knives commonly found around and through it. Releasing the heart sometimes takes an entire session in itself, and might need the conscious cooperation of the client before it will release. It may have separated itself from the client to protect the client from the grief it holds. The client may need to reassure the heart that he is willing to deal with any ensuing grief and pain in an attempt to transmute it. He may need to ask the heart to permit the release of all walls, chains and other devices, so that they can be removed. Removal of walls and chains is described under "Removal of Implants and Devices."

Some other areas of release that I address a little differently, are the meridians and the nervous system. Both may be addressed as described earlier, but to the meridians you may add:

"I ask you to become strong, wide, and follow your proper course."

The nerves are usually totally frazzled! Besides the routine release, I ask that

"all excess energy on the nerves be released, now."

For type A individuals, releasing excess energy from the nerves can be massive! Create an etheric salve of blue-green color and coat the nerves to soothe and calm the nerve ends. Clients frequently comment on how comforting this feels.

In dealing with forms of consciousness having "bodies" such as parasites, bacteria, or fungus, try talking to their individual oversoul. For a person suffering with parasitic worms (very common), join with the consciousness of the oversoul of the parasites. Explain the concept of consciousness-raising on the planet, and ask if it would be willing to speed its evolution by progressing from a parasite, which is causing harm to this physical body, to a higher form of consciousness such as an earthworm. If it says yes, ask if it would draw the life force, or intelligences, from the parasites back to itself. Ask that the parasite bodies, larvae and spores be dissolved. When working with parasites, prepare the client to undergo a healing crisis. If the parasitic energies are not totally removed, the parasites may reinfest. To pull the energy of the parasites from the aura, it is preferable for the client to soak in one-half cup of Clorox brand bleach in a tub of water, for twenty minutes, three times a week. Some people are sensitive to bleach, however, so you could muscle check, using kinesiology, to determine if bleach is acceptable, how much to use and how often. If there are any doubts, play it safe and suggest sea salt only.

RELEASE OF UNDESIRABLE AND PARASITIC ENERGIES

Of the unreal, there is no existence.
Of the real, there is no nonexistence.
The final truth of both of these is know by men of wisdom.

— Bhagavad Gita

All techniques from now on will be done with the assistance of Archangel Michael and the angelic realm. Begin your session having first invoked them, along with any spiritual guides to whom you may feel drawn. It is suggested that you have a clear understanding of these parasitic energies, described under "Part II: The Spiritual Warrior," before attempting the following techniques.

RELEASE OF CREATURES

These etheric insects, snakes and other reptiles are almost always uncooperative. They have no concept of a person's free will. Their only concern is to exist.

The following is an example of a creature who was attached to one of my clients. We found a huge etheric worm in her intestines. Upon being discovered, and angered that it was asked to leave, it turned into thousands of worms which swarmed in her stomach, causing nausea and gagging. I immediately encapsulated the worms, while I grabbed a trash can for her to vomit into. As I continued my release process, the worms were removed and the client regained her stomach (never having vomited, thank goodness!).

When discovering a "creature," have the Light beings encapsulate it in Light. Ask that the energy (the creature) be transmuted to a higher consciousness. If the creature is of a very unsophisticated intelligence, it may actually disintegrate into a "poof" of energy and be gone. If this doesn't happen, ask that it be taken to its appropriate place in the Light. At that point, you should see it removed. Be sure that the creature is totally gone from your sight. If it merely moves to the periphery of your vision, something remains to be done. I often find at such times that the energy has not been broken between it and the client; there may be an etheric thread connecting the two. Create a violet flame of transmuting fire or Michael's flaming blue sword which can be created with your intention — see it or ask for it. See the flame burn the space between the client and the object or creature. Once the connection is cut, the object should then be removed from your sight.

After removing an object from a person's energy field, check for any holes that may have been left in the aura. Attachments are parasitic and live within and on a person's energy body, so when attachments are removed, sometimes areas of the person's field go along. A hole may do as much acute damage as the attachment did over a long period. Repair the hole using the process described in "Repairing Auric Holes and Rips." Then ask that,

"All bodies go into their proper spacing and integrate."

Next, ask the healing angels to repair what can be repaired. Color is also very useful. I frequently ask the blue and green rays to penetrate and soothe all cells that would benefit from them. Different colors may be appropriate for your client, so use your intuition.

RELEASE OF NEGATIVE THOUGHT FORMS

These are the energies that we create by our thoughts. Treat them as you would any intelligence which has served a purpose in the past, but is no longer useful. A two-way conversation with these is rarely necessary as they leave very easily. Encapsulate them in Light and say,

"I ask that these negative thought forms leave John, now. I ask that they be transmuted to a higher energy, now."

Then state,

"I ask that all negative ancient thought forms be released now and be transmuted to a higher energy, now."

The term "ancient thought form" seems to release at a much deeper level, though it doesn't seem to work well unless the regular thought forms have been released first.

RELEASE OF THOUGHT FORM MONSTERS AND ASTRAL MONSTER PROJECTILES

These powerful thought forms, which take on a life of their own, are the nastiest of all dark energies other than the Dark Forces. They can cause tremendous harm to the client, usually physically, and are very unpleasant about leaving. Other than snarling and growling, these monsters do not communicate as they have no intelligence of their own. They often appear very similar to Dark Forces. If you have doubts as to what you are dealing with, use the release method for Dark Forces. Otherwise, use the following technique: Call Archangel Michael's angels to encapsulate them. This is a strong, impenetrable capsule of Light which the monsters are unable to break through. Ask the angels to have the monsters and projectiles removed to their appropriate place in the Light. You will almost always have to use the violet flame or the flaming blue sword to cut any energy attachments, then repair any holes using an etheric crystal (Described under "Repairing Auric Holes and Rips"). Ask the angels to repair what can be repaired. Saturate the cells with blue-green by calling the intelligent rays of the colors blue and green. See these colors penetrate the client's bodies.

REMOVAL OF IMPLANTS AND DEVICES

Devices are walls, cages, or other objects anywhere within the aura, frequently seen around the heart. When you discover such devices, you may ask them what purpose they serve the client. The implants are usually small and shaped like a box, tube or spiral. They are frequently seen within the spinal column, around the pituitary and in the rectum, but they can be anywhere. Both implants and devices are rarely hostile or aggressive, and usually communicate willingly; however, they are not always willing to leave, as they may still be serving a purpose to your client. When in doubt, call the client's higher Self. Ask the higher Self what the appropriate action should be. Then trust your answer and proceed with your session.

To remove any device or object, ask that it be surrounded in golden Light and then sense or see it removed or dissolved. Sometimes it's that simple. Other times more effort on your part is needed; you may have to remove it yourself. To do this, see an impenetrable golden glove on your hand. Remove the object with the glove and hand it to an angel who will take it to its appropriate place. When removing objects, remember to look for a remaining hole in the person's field and repair it (described under "Repairing Auric Holes and Rips"). Implants are to be handled in the same manner. If looking specifically for an implant, simply state that as your intention and begin looking.

An example of such devices occurred during an in-person session with one of my clients. We found a stake through her heart, a piece of her heart missing, and a dark shadow around the heart. The stake had been put there by a medicine man many lifetimes ago. It was meant to literally hold together a heart which had been broken in two. I wondered if it would be wise to remove the stake, so I called to her higher Self and our angelic guidance. We were told that her heart had mended enough to remove the stake, which we then did. As for the missing piece, I would ordinarily have found it and reintegrated it back into the whole. However, we were told that she was not ready to bring the pain (which the missing piece represented) back. The dark ring around the heart was put there to separate the pain of the heart from her conscious mind. She was also not ready to heal this. The client and I then discussed what this meant to her. She admitted that she was not yet ready to heal on such a deep level. This describes a situation in which one device (stake) was removed, while another device (dark ring) and a fragmented heart were not to be disturbed.

To summarize the release of creatures, thought forms, implants and devices:
- Invoke your guidance and that of your client, healing angels of Light, Archangel Michael and his band of angels.
- Discover purpose of nasty, implant or device, if possible.
- Encapsulate with Light.
- Ask that it be taken to its appropriate place in the Light, or see it dissolve.
- Put on golden glove and remove, if appropriate.
- Use violet flame or flaming blue sword to cut energy link.
- Repair holes.
- Ask healing angels to repair what can be repaired.
- Saturate cells with blue-green light, if appropriate.
- Thank all beings of Light who helped in the session.

INTEGRATING MIND/SOUL FRAGMENTS OR "SOUL RETRIEVAL"

Fragmentation occurs when a portion of a person's consciousness breaks away, leaving the person unwhole and scattered. To find and reintegrate the fragment, scan the client, looking for etheric cords, bands, threads, or holes with bands extending from them. Follow these to their ends where you should find a "personality" — the fragment that split from the whole consciousness. The fragment will almost always be either afraid or angry — displaying the emotion that initially caused the fragmentation. It will have been frozen in time at the moment of fragmenting and will still be of that same age, with no memory beyond the time when the actual split took place. The process of reintegration is to reassure and convince the fragment that it's okay to return.

Here is a sample dialogue to the fragment:

"Look at Susie (the client). See; she's all grown up and doing fine. She really misses you. She's okay now. She really needs you to come back so that she can become whole again. Don't you want to go home to her now? (If it is convinced that it's safe, it will be anxious to reintegrate.) I ask the angels of Light to surround this fragment, escort it back along it's cord, and reintegrate it with Susie."

See or sense the fragment reintegrate.

When you scan a client, you might also find a personality that is actually an attached discarnate or an attached fragment from someone else. Talk to it and get its history. This way you can differentiate a discarnate from a fragment. If your client has an attached fragment from someone else, I suggest that you ask its name and why it is with your client, as it will almost always be someone your client knows. Ask the angels of Light to escort the fragment back to its own consciousness, after reassuring the fragment that it is now safe to return. If you discover that you're dealing with an attached discarnate, follow the release procedure described in the following section.

To summarize the procedure for reintegrating mind/soul fragments or "soul retrieval:"
- Invoke your client's guidance, healing angels of Light, Archangel Michael and his band of angels.
- Ask the name of fragment and why it fragmented, if applicable.
- Reassure the fragment that it is safe to return to its whole.
- Ask Light beings to escort the fragment back to its whole and be reintegrated.
- Thank all Light beings who helped.

RELEASE OF EARTHBOUND DISCARNATES

Unless a discarnate presents itself to me, I rarely release it until I have released the Dark Forces first. Dark Forces intend to prevent everyone from making spiritual progress, so they frequently interfere with the release of discarnates, which can make your work needlessly complicated. If a Dark Force does interfere, he will need to be released before you continue — best to get them out of the way, first.

To discover discarnates, as you scan your client's body notice any faces or personalities that may wish to talk to you, or may just be observing you; these will most often be discarnates. If your client is concerned that a deceased person she knew may be attached to her, you can call the name of the deceased. If the deceased is an attachment, he will be so shocked to be spoken to, that he will almost always answer. You may also demand or intend to see any and all discarnates that are attached to your client, and they will appear.

As you speak to discarnates, remember that they are totally confused, always scared and usually distrustful. Some won't speak to you other than to tell you to leave them alone. Others are thrilled to be recognized and will chatter forever, given the chance. For the client's benefit, you may choose to ask them how it is that they came to attach to your client, when they attached, and what influence they have over your client.

When listening to discarnates, do not be gullible. Just because a person is dead does not mean he is enlightened, and what he says to you may not be the truth at all. If the discarnate was a prankster in life, he will be a prankster still, in his current earthbound state. A discarnate may profess not to be a discarnate at all, but an angel or spirit guide. Use your common sense here. This is particularly important should you need to distinguish a guide or deceased loved one from an earthbound discarnate. No being from the Light is attached to anyone's energy field. Light beings also don't chatter away just to make conversation. I have known far too many professed "channelers" who channeled earthbound discarnates, thinking they were beings from the higher realms. Use your intuition. If you encounter a personality, and you question if it is from the Light or not, ask it to enter the Light. A true Light being will respect your wishes. An earthbound discarnate or a being from the dark will either refuse or not know what you're talking about.

The first step in releasing a discarnate is to educate him. A sample conversation is as follows:

"At some point you lost your physical body. This, as you know it, is called death. All humans, no matter what their religious belief, have a period of rest after they lose their physical bodies. When you died there appeared a bright light near you. This light was your entrance to that rest, but for whatever reason, you did not go to it. If you had entered that light, you would be able to prepare another physical body for yourself. Wouldn't you love to have your own body again, instead of having to live through, and share someone else's?" (This gives the strongest impetus for them to leave their host and enter the Light.)

"All people, no matter how good or bad they were in life, and no matter what their religion or lack of it, are given this opportunity after losing their physical body. I now bring this light to you again so that you may be rescued from your present state of limbo." (Whether they're ready to go or not, see the Light engulf your client.)

"I ask a loved one from the Light, or an angelic being from the Light, to take this discarnate by the hand and escort him into the Light."

Frequently a beloved relative or friend will come to the discarnate. It's a blessed relief for him, and can be a very heartwarming sight as he rejoins with someone he loves, and is finally rescued from his purgatory.

It is possible to do a mass release of discarnates, preferably after all Dark Forces have been removed. Mass release is advantageous in that all attached earth bound souls are released at once. However, since there is no individual communication with the discarnates, it is not elucidating for the client as no informative conversation occurs.

To perform a mass release of discarnates, see your client before you. State:

"To all of you who are with Mary and have lost your physical body: Listen to what I have to say."

Then continue the dialogue as previously described. It is not necessary to address the discarnates individually. Call the Light beings to take them by the hand and escort them into the Light. You may be shocked by the number of discarnates that can rise from one client.

Both released discarnates, and Dark Forces, may take huge areas of the client's energy field with them, since their field and the client's had meshed. Look for, and then mend, any holes (described under "Repairing Auric Holes and Rips"). Ask the healing angels to repair what can be repaired. Soothe the cells with the blue and green rays, or make an etheric blue-green salve, if you feel that it is necessary. Released entities may leave behind a residue of etheric sludge which should be removed by doing a thorough aura cleaning. Take advantage of the cleaning and do yourself at the same time. To clean the aura, see a white/gold tornado, about ten feet around, coming down from above. See it move down through the head, bodies and energy field. The strength and twirl of this tornado is extremely powerful and is maintained with your intention and concentration. It often vibrates the body as it passes through. When finished, see the tornado go into the ground or into the sky, intending that the energy be transmuted. Depending on how dirty the client's field is, you may have to do this up to three times. After cleaning the aura, saturate the bodies with golden Light; sense the Light as it heals and rejuvenates every cell and atom.

If a woman has had a miscarriage or abortion, the entity will often attach in her pelvic region, as the fetus literally holds onto the mother for life. War veterans, hospital employees, street drug and alcohol abusers, and sexually indiscriminate people usually have more than their share of discarnate attachments; however, everyone will have them to some degree.

Some people believe that by simply commanding a discarnate into the Light, it will go. This idea stems from incomplete knowledge of the nature of discarnates. If someone commanded you to jump into a white tunnel, would you do it simply because you were commanded? Probably not, unless you already knew why this would benefit you. A discarnate reasons like you would; he is just a person without a physical body. For this reason, commanding them into the Light without prior explanation has very limited success. Remember, they already had a chance to enter it and didn't, so for them to agree to enter now may take some educating on your part. After all, why should they trust you? We living beings may think of the Light as a wonderful place to be, but to a discarnate it could be perceived quite differently. You'll find that many discarnates are afraid of the Light for various reasons. Some may think you're trying to trick them and that the Light may actually be a worse place than where they presently are. This is why you should call a loved one from the Light to escort them. Angels frequently overwhelm the discarnates by their very magnitude and brilliance, therefore a loved one is preferred and an angel would be the second choice for an escort. You may also encounter a discarnate who feels unworthy to go to "heaven." Assure him that this place of rest (the Light) is for everyone that loses his physical body, regardless of his past deeds. Then ask,

"If you are so unworthy, would an angel bestow his presence upon you?"

Next call an angel of Light to come forward. If he believes in heaven, he will probably be awed by the presence of an angel. Of course, this would not work with a person who is overwhelmed by an angel.

It all boils down to using your common sense. Put yourself in their shoes and try to really understand them. In the successful release of discarnates, you are likely to encounter some very wonderful, heart warming experiences as these distressed beings are rescued from their confusion and grief and set free to continue their spiritual journey.

To summarize release of earthbound discarnates:
- Call your spiritual guidance and your client's, also Archangel Michael and his angels, to stand by and hold off any darkness that may interfere.
- See/sense all discarnates who are with the client.
- Obtain history of discarnates, if desired, and educate them about their present condition.
- Ask Light beings to take them by the hand and escort them to the Light.

- Look for holes and repair.
- Ask angels to repair what can be repaired.
- Saturate cells with blue-green if necessary.
- Clean aura with a white/golden tornado.
- Saturate the bodies with golden Light.
- Thank all beings who assisted.

RELEASE OF THE DARK FORCES

If an angel of Light had all his light removed, he would be an angel of darkness. With no Light, he would not know love or compassion as it simply would not exist for him. However, deep down underneath all that blackness, there would still be a remaining spark of Light from his original source. This is the situation with the Dark Forces.

It is important to understand that the Dark Forces have no intention of returning to the Light. Except for the very highest order of Dark Forces, they believe there is no Light in them, and that prolonged exposure to the Light will burn them. We have a few tricks to convince them otherwise, but they also have a few of their own. One of their tricks involves assuming various shapes and forms. Although to a clairvoyant eye they usually appear as blobs of black energy, as they never had a physical body and have never been human, they can temporarily transform their appearance. The shapes, or "masks" that they don, are designed to induce fear, because fear creates a vibration that they can control. Common masks they use are those of a spider, Grim Reaper, dragon, gargoyle, and snake. If they pull this trick on you, simply command them to take their masks off. They will be so shocked at the confrontation that they will usually obey.

Since their energy fields are so strong, they can also transform themselves into beings of Light to deceive you. However, they cannot hold the Light very long and will soon return to their black demeanor. If you should ever question (please do question!) whether you are truly speaking to a Light being, ask to see his eyes. If he turns his head away from you or leaves, then you can be certain he is not from the Light. A Dark Force will avert his eyes because they are red. In addition, even though he may transform himself into a Light being for a short while (not more than a few minutes) he will never radiate the warmth of a true being from the Light. His demeanor and vibration will always be cold.

Another trick of the Dark Forces is the use of very foul language. They can curse profusely and be extremely belligerent. This tactic is, of course, designed to catch you off guard and put you on the defensive. It might also create anger and resistance in you, which lowers your defenses and makes you more susceptible to their influence. If they spout offensive language at you, simply tell them to be quiet; you don't want to hear it.

Projecting evil energy towards you is another means of control they use. To call it evil is accurate, to say the least, but don't let it scare you (which, of course, is what it's meant to do). Remind them that you know, and you know that they know, that Archangel Michael and his angels are surrounding you, and that the strength of these angels of Light is much more powerful than their evil. "So cut it out!"

Whatever you experience — and I cannot emphasize this enough — never, ever take any of the following attitudes: fighting, going to war, getting the best of them, or FEAR! These are the realms in which they are empowered. We want to function from the areas that empower us, which are love and spiritual strength.

You'll notice as you do this work, that the angels of Light do not "go against" their dark brothers. They create no resistance, but merely stand around them, and subdue them with total calm. This shows once again that, from a higher viewpoint, the Light and dark are co-creators.

The Dark Forces have a hierarchy, as do the angels of Light. Satan is an archangel of the dark. He reigns over a continuum of lower ranks, each being accountable to the one above. The dark angels begin in the lower ranks and "evolve up," gaining in power, strength and size. Each of the dark brothers also has a counterpart Light angel. You might consider his counterpart to be his true essence before he chose to serve the dark. The counterpart reflects his true identity.

Regarding the consciousness of the Dark Forces: They believe that they are not part of the Light, and that the Light will burn them. They also have complete and total allegiance to their superiors and are convinced that if they fail in their mission they will be tortured. Their one-pointed goal is to bring ruin and destruction. They make promises which they never keep. Moral ethics do not exist to them, and they do not understand compassion or love.

The Dark Forces have played a major role in the evolution of humanity, and they will remain on Earth until mass consciousness is no longer in need of their lessons. We know that the time for learning lessons is just about over. Whether humanity is ready or not, Earth is undergoing a tremendous transformation into a planet of Light. All who wish to live on her will have to keep pace with her new vibration. The new humanity and new Earth will no longer be under the influence of the Dark Forces, as is the case now. So, just as the pain and grief which we hold in our cells no longer serve us, neither do the Dark Forces. (I must clarify that I am speaking in generalities here. As stated earlier, some people still need the pain or the Dark Forces, because they have not yet completed some particular experience for their soul growth.)

The transmutation now taking place is not just about humans and the planet, however, but about all intelligences that are affected by this particular reality we call "living on Earth." This includes a transmutation of the Dark Forces as well. As humans accepted the illusion of separation from their divine identity, so have the Dark Forces. They have forgotten their original nature of Light, and now is the time for them to remember. Soon there will be no place for them on this planet, so they may either return to the Light, or continue their work somewhere else. However, as is the case with humans, not every Dark Force is ready to return.

The higher-ranking ones know the truth of their origin, and know that their time here is short-lived. They are also aware that the Earth's transmutation to a higher vibration *will* take place regardless of their actions, yet they are still orchestrating chaos on Earth and trying to create so much destruction and hate among the inhabitants of this planet, that a transmutation cannot take place. They will do anything they can to hinder individuals from raising their consciousness. This is their last stand, you might say. And those individuals who succumb to their pressure and cannot resonate to the new vibration on Earth, will be reborn on another planet where they will continue their growth. The lower-ranked ones, which are the ones that attach to humans, are the ones I return to the Light.

Let me relate an encounter I had with a high-ranking Dark Force who was not ready to return to the Light. I was doing a remote session on a client, had encapsulated her Dark Forces, when a HUGE Dark Force and his army suddenly appeared to the left of my field of vision. I immediately asked the angels of Light to encapsulate him, but nothing happened. I knew, somehow, that he knew everything I was going to do and was actually one step ahead of me. He had a powerful, quiet demeanor, very different from the mouthy ones I had become accustomed to. I found myself in awe of his manner but also leery of it, especially since he was not encapsulated. As I was processing the situation and considering what to do, a Master came between this dark giant and me. They carried on a conversation to which I was not privy. After a few minutes, the dark being turned and, with army in tow, departed. The Master then instructed me to continue the process with my client, and left.

This huge dark being knew what was happening. There was nothing I could have told him and nothing I could have done with him. He was continuing to orchestrate his realm of darkness, and for him, it wasn't over yet. However, the underlings, as in most military structures, haven't a clue; they simply obey orders. These lesser ones are the ones you will usually encounter, but be prepared for the others. I have frequently encountered Dark Forces who say they know they are of the Light, but choose not to return. In truth, they *do not* know that they are of the Light, but say this in hopes of deceiving me. They claim my "tricks" won't work on them. This is really one of their tricks to catch me off guard. If this should happen to you, encapsulate the dark one immediately. If the angels of Light hold him bound, continue your process. Notice his amazement when he finds out that he *really is* of the Light!

As you come in contact with Dark Forces, you absolutely must not project emotions onto them, such as anger, fear, sympathy, or even love. Understand that these powerful beings are composed of pure energy, and are masters at converting energy for their use. Emotion is the prime energy with which they have manipulated and controlled people for eons. You might think that sending them white Light or love would soften them. Remember, as mentioned earlier, that white Light is unconditional and therefore can be manipulated and used for various purposes. Also, be aware that Dark Forces can transform themselves into angels of Light. This takes tremendous amounts of energy on their part, but they are able to do it. As for sending them love, the non-ascended human is not yet able to radiate perfect unconditional love; it almost always contains an element of emotion such as sympathy, desire, or a touch of pain. Any such emotion can be twisted back on the projector or used to strengthen the dark one. A being can only experience that which is part of its reality, and the Dark Forces have no sense of love in theirs. To them, it simply does not exist.

One would think that, since they stemmed from angels of Light, they must have a spark of Light or God essence somewhere within. Yes, they do, but it is no more than smoldering ash laying dormant, buried under so many layers of blackness that to them it does not exist. Only when they remember what they were before they embraced the darkness does the Light begin to revitalize. At that point they begin to feel shame and sorrow for their deeds and feel the love vibration from the angels of Light.

The attitude that must be assumed when working with the Dark Forces is that of steady, unwavering indifference. Neutral. Only after the process of their transmutation is completed, can you leap for joy at the wonderful service that you have just performed.

Two techniques that have been used in the past to remove Dark Forces, were to command them gone in the name of Jesus Christ and/or recite the Lord's Prayer. This works to a degree if a Dark Force is around you, but almost never works if it is attached to you. If you should feel the evil presence of a dark being hovering around, and you command him away in the name of the Lord Jesus Christ, he probably will leave for a short time and then return. I have also known them not to leave at all. In either case, you have only temporarily solved the problem as they are still free to continue harassing you, or someone else. This technique also provides no service to them or their armies as they were not educated nor returned to the Light.

The process that I have been given to release Dark Forces is as follows: I ask for protection, and call in Archangel Michael and his angels, and all relevant spiritual guidance. I ask for Michael's flaming blue sword to guard me and then etherically call up my client. If I don't immediately see her Dark Forces, I command them to show themselves. I then see several black blobs staring threateningly at me. Typically the numbers range from four to six in the average adult, though I've seen up to eleven in a Vietnam veteran, and as few as two in a child. There will usually be one Dark Force of higher position than the others. He is the one that will take the lead in communicating with you. You can direct your statements to him, but you are actually addressing all of them. I ask the angels to encapsulate all Dark Forces. When I see this done I explain to them what I'm doing. The dialogue moves very quickly with you doing most of the talking. The point is to get them to think and to listen to you. I have the ability to turn my hearing on and off. When working with Dark Forces I usually leave it off, as their belligerent cursing can be disarming. When they realize that I am not hearing them, they settle down. Once I sense that they have realized their true origin, I turn my hearing back on.

The gist of the dialogue is as follows:

"I have something to explain to you. You have been lied to about your identity; you've been deceived. You've been told that you are of the darkness and must serve it. You've been told that you have no light in you and that prolonged exposure to the light will burn you. Notice whether the light is burning you now." (Remember, they're encapsulated with light.)

"What's happening to your edges? Are you burning?" (The edges will eventually begin to grow lighter.)

"Look inside yourself, deep under all that blackness. What do you see?" (Eventually they will see a spark of color. It will grow with attention drawn to it. You're not really expecting an answer from all these questions; you're just getting them to think.)

"There was a time when you had a purpose serving the darkness, but that time is over, now. You do not have much time left on this planet. Because your time will soon be over, I'm going to remove the lie that was perpetrated upon you. What's happening to your edges, now? Are you burning?" (Mentioning their edges is just to keep them paying attention and in a state of upheaval, especially when they realize they're not burning. It creates doubt within them.)

"You have not always served the darkness. Remember the time before you gave your allegiance to the darkness. What were you then?" (By now they're usually thinking that you might have some credibility since they're not burning yet.)

"Think far, far back. What were you? I now call Archangel Michael to remove the veil of memory from these dark ones." (Removing the veil of memory lifts the amnesia that separates them from remembering their true identities. You will see, or have a sense of an energy shift. Wait a while, maybe two minutes, as the dark ones begin to remember.)

"Do you remember, now? Do you see how you've been lied to?" (They are usually stunned to silence at this point.)

"Look at your middle again. See the light within you?" (By now it's visible, and they can't deny it.)

"What are you going to do now? You can't go back and serve the dark. They don't want you; you have light in you! And staying where you are (attached to the client) **is not an option. I'll give you a way out. You can serve your true identity. I call from the Light, the counterparts of these dark ones."** (This part is truly fascinating! The counterparts come forward and stand before their dark brothers. The counterpart is the exact opposite and yet the same being as each dark one. Think of it as identical twins separated at birth, in which one becomes a saint and the other becomes evil. So when the dark one meets its counterpart, it recognizes itself, but as a being of Light instead of dark. The dark ones are also now able to tolerate more Light, and for the first time in eons, feel the love vibration. As they recognize their counterparts, the realization is sometimes almost overwhelming. I've seen them touch their counterparts with such relief, as if an eternity of burden has just been lifted from them.)

"This is your true identity. You may go with them to a place of rest and healing. You will then serve with them, maintaining even more power and strength than you have now, but that strength and power will be used for the Light. Are you ready to go with these, your brothers, to the Light?" (They almost always say "yes." If not, give them a little more time to integrate what they've just learned. The only choice they actually have, at this point, is to go to the Light. Remind them that if they try to go back to the darkness, they will be tortured for having failed in their assignment, or at least, this is what they believe. Also remind them that staying where they are is not an option).

At this point they often have fears that the dark will capture and punish them before they can get to the Light. You can reassure them by saying,

"You are protected now by the Light and these Light beings. The dark can not harm you as long as you are willing to serve your true identity of Light."

Then say,

"You realize that you have a karmic debt to pay for all the pain you've inflicted, don't you?" (Here they always cringe.)

"Would you like to lessen that debt?" (A unanimous "yes" every time.)

"Then I ask that you call to you now, all your underlings and equals, from all the galaxies and all the dimensions, past, present and future." (This can be somewhat frightful. The sky and surroundings will become totally blackened by the Dark Forces answering the call. They will gather around your client, coming from the oceans, sky and earth. If you feel the projection of their evil, or feel yourself becoming overwhelmed by their numbers, remember that you are strongly protected and that the Light outnumbers the dark two to one.)

"Angels of Light, encapsulate all who come." (Wait until no more come and they are all encapsulated.) "Command all underlings and equals to follow you."

"Now I ask you to pull in and absorb back into yourselves all your projections and projectiles, from all the galaxies and dimensions, from the past, present and future." (Projections are thought projections or negative thought forms. Projectiles are actual extensions of a Dark Force which he has attached to someone or something. By so doing, one Dark Force can influence many individuals while preserving the main portion of himself, and therefore the greatest amount of his energy.)

"I ask that you command all these underlings and equals to do the same." (Wait until you feel it is done.)

"Are you ready to go to the Light?" (They're ready!)

"I ask the angels of Light to take these dark beings to their appropriate place in the Light." (Some of the Dark Forces will actually be totally possessed E.T.'s who had not been able to separate their own identities from their Dark Force possession. Their "Light" is sometimes different from ours. Where ours is white, I've seen theirs to be orange. It all depends on their planetary origin. We really don't know where "the appropriate place in the Light" is for them, so we simply state it, knowing they will be taken to a suitable place for their highest good.)

At some time during your session you may become aware of another dark being who just seemed to show up. He is usually quite large and is the commander of the ones to whom you are speaking. He'll usually say something like, "What do you think you're doing?!" Encapsulate him and begin your process from the beginning, speaking now to this commander as your Dark Force representative. The higher in rank, the more you can release and rescue.

Occasionally a Dark Force is not restrained by the Light sent to encapsulate him. Should this occur, send a quick mental thought for Archangel Michael himself to help you. The being will be restrained and you can then continue your process. If you have called for Archangel Michael's flaming blue sword, and have positioned it in front of you, know for certain that you will not be harmed, no matter how loose, free and aggressive a Dark Force may be. He can only bluff. He knows he cannot harm you, but he will do everything he can to make you think otherwise.

After releasing the Dark Forces, I concentrate next on the discarnates. I do a mass discarnate release as described earlier. If you should choose to do an individual release of either Dark Forces or discarnates, understand that if they don't want to be known, they will hide. This means that they will be silent and try not to be seen. They might also hop out of the client, deceiving you into thinking that they have been released, then hop back in later. For these reasons, mass release is preferred for all Dark Forces and discarnates. By asking that the Dark Forces be encapsulated, you ensure that they all will be. They cannot hide from the angels of Light. For the discarnates, even though you may not see every one of them, when you call for a loved one or angel of Light to come forward, all will be approached. This is very important, especially when clearing large areas of Dark Forces or discarnates in which there are too many for you to keep track of or notice. This might be the case in clearing large buildings such as hospitals or apartment buildings, or in clearing land.

To summarize Dark Force releasement:
• Call Archangel Michael and his band of angels.
• Place Michael's flaming blue sword in front of you.
• Call your spiritual guidance and that of your client.
• Call up your client and have all Dark Forces encapsulated.
• Converse as described.
• Have Archangel Michael remove the veil of memory.
• Call counterparts.
• Call all of equal and lesser rank and encapsulate.
• Pull in all projections and projectiles.

- Remove all to their appropriate place in the Light.
- Ask healing angels to heal what can be healed.
- Saturate cells with blue-green light.
- Look for auric holes and repair.
- Use white/gold tornado to thoroughly clean aura and any remaining etheric sludge.
- Saturate the bodies with golden Light.

The book *Dark Robes, Dark Brothers* by Hilarion, mentions contracts or agreements made between the beings of dark and the beings of Light regarding a particular person. By allowing the Dark Forces to create temporary hardships for an individual, an agreement is made in which the forces of Light can then assist one who would ordinarily be under the influence of the darkness. These agreements can be broken. If you suspect that you are under the influence of such a contract, you have the ability to terminate it. The process goes as follows:

"I speak to the beings of the dark and the beings of the Light." (See, or imagine, the light and dark standing opposite to each other.)

"I exert my right of free will and state that the contract you have on me is broken now!"

Then raise Michael's sword and slam through the space between the two forces. When I do this, I see that I have cut the center of an etheric cord; half of it goes back to the Light and half goes back to the dark. When doing this on behalf of someone else, use the same technique, but preface it by stating,

"On behalf of John, who chooses to exert his free will, this contract is now broken!"

Dark Robes, Dark Brothers explains this process of contracts in detail and thoroughly discusses Dark Forces. I suggest that you do not break a contract without understanding what the contract states and why it exists, as you may find that the benefits outweigh the temporary hardships. Neither should you break someone else's contract without first receiving permission from their spiritual guidance or higher Self.

CLEARING HOUSES AND BUILDINGS

Whenever I move into a new house, stay in a hotel room, or stay in somebody else's home, I first do a good etheric cleaning of the place. Before I became aware of the etheric realms, I lived in many houses in which I was simply miserable, but never knew why. I had a feeling of anxiety as I crossed the threshold. It just didn't "feel" good. Now, of course, I understand that I was feeling the remnant energies of all the people who had lived there before me — their emotions of sadness and anger. I'm sure I also felt the energy of scared discarnate beings and even Dark Forces who dwelled within these houses.

When you were a child, were you afraid of the dark or afraid to go to sleep at night? Did you fear horrible things under the bed and in the closet, or did you know other children who did? Children do not create fears out of nowhere unless they watch the wrong type of television shows. (In fact, if they watch any television these days, they can go into fear!) But a young child, who is "irrationally" scared, usually has a reason. Children don't rationalize away their feelings like adults tend to do. If a child is scared in his room at night, there's probably something there that is scaring him. He "feels" something scary. Many times I have cleared a child's room only to find a discarnate hiding in the closet and gobs of dark energy under the bed or in the corners. Once the room is cleared, the fear is gone.

You don't have to be knowledgeable in releasing discarnates or Dark Forces to clean a house; however, if you are not, and you run across one, you'll have to ignore him. So, it is best to be adept at all releasement work so that you can take care of whatever may come up.

There are many ways of clearing energy, but I have never found any to be as powerful as the white/gold tornado. First call Archangel Michael and his band of angels. Ask them to stand by in case you need them. Release any entities you find using the technique described. Then create a white/gold tornado — about ten feet wide. Control its speed and power with your intention. See the tornado come down from the sky and enter at one end of the house or building. Have it move up and down in each room, thoroughly cleaning through all closets, corners, inside drawers and shelves, under beds, around toilets, through couches and bookshelves. See it move through the walls and continue room by room. Scan the house, making sure that it feels good and that there's no lingering dirty energy. Repeat the process if necessary. When you're finished, have the tornado either go into the ground or back into the sky. Intend that the energy be transmuted for a higher use.

How thoroughly a job is done depends on you. If the building has never been etherically cleaned and you just zip through it, then a lot of dirty energy will remain in closed areas such as corners and closets. However, after doing a thorough cleaning the first time, a "zip through" every now and then is all that's needed to maintain a high energy, good-feeling house.

HEALING CHILDREN

When we humans incarnate, we bring a certain amount of karma that needs to be resolved. By releasing Dark Forces and performing Cellular Memory

Release, we are actually releasing the client from the karma that he would ordinarily have to experience. We can do this only because a divine dispensation for the absolution of karma has been granted to Earth at this time. It is also allowed because those who we release have already experienced a necessary part of their karma and are ready to clear themselves for their spiritual work. Remember, however, that if one is holding certain karma that is still necessary for a while, the healing will not take place. Children have experienced almost no karma in their short Earth years, therefore considerable discretion is needed when doing cellular or attachment release on kids. Even though you have permission from the parent, you must contact the child's higher Self for permission as well. From my personal experience, the higher Self, on frequent occasions, has refused me permission to perform cellular release or release of Dark Forces on children under fifteen. Reiki and other modes of healing may be quite appropriate, but the techniques described in this book go far beyond simple healing energy. Definitely listen to your higher guidance when working with children.

HEALING ANIMALS

Believe it or not, animals get attachments — not by discarnate people, but by discarnate animals. True story: I can count the times my twelve-year-old cat has presented me with a half mangled, dead animal. She has always been happy and well-fed, and never had much of a hunting spirit about her, so killing little critters was not something she usually did. But when, within one week, she brought home two dead gophers, a mangled mole and three half eaten birds, I knew something was amiss. Other than this, her behavior had not changed. I went into a meditative state, called her up (etherically) in front of me and scanned her. What I was doing was a remote session on my cat, just as I would a client. What I found was a huge astral snake. This was not a "creature" as described earlier, but an actual dead snake. I called Archangel Michael to encapsulate and remove it. I used the violet flame to purge any residue energy, saw no rips or holes in her aura, and that was all it took. She never brought me any more trophies after that.

I have released snakes, coyotes, birds and Dark Forces from animals. For anything other than the Dark Forces, simply call Archangel Michael and have them encapsulated and removed. There's no conversation involved. However, if they have a Dark Force attached, use the technique described earlier for Dark Forces. All Dark Forces, no matter what they're attached to, are still Dark Forces and need to be removed in the same manner. If an animal has been traumatized by his attachments, check if he has left his body. If he has, you'll notice that part of his consciousness is hovering over the physical. Speak to the consciousness and encourage it to reintegrate. If an animal becomes ill or has a sudden change of personality, check for attachments. Animals do well with Cellular Memory Release and are sponges for Reiki and Magnified Healing energy, also.

Many people do not realize that their animal friends absorb a lot of their energy. This is one of the reasons why animals, especially domestic ones, are so healing; they actually take away our physical and emotional pain. Unfortunately, when they do this they absorb those energies into themselves. Many animals have the same ailments as do their people. If you have never considered this point, and you have a domestic animal friend, think about the times that you have felt glum or happy, and your animal felt the same. Notice if your animal, curiously, has the same physical problems as you. You can save your animal and yourself trips to the vet by simply releasing energies that do not belong to her. Join with her consciousness and state, "All energies that are not yours, leave now." Do this a couple of times until no more release. See the energy go into a golden light or a violet flame. You may also have a talk with the animal's consciousness stating that you take responsibility for your own heavy energies and that she does not need to absorb them. My personal experience with this began when my cat's right eye started watering. I kept looking to see what was in it but found no cause for the condition. I did Reiki and other healing techniques, but nothing seemed to work. One day I was having trouble with allergies and my eyes were watering and stinging. I realized that her eyes were watering the same way mine often had. That's when it struck me that she had picked up my allergies. I released her of my energies and her eyes stopped watering.

RELEASING LAND

Earlier I wrote of holding and anchoring Light into the earth, especially at vortexes and ley lines. Those of us who do release work may be asked to go a step further and actually clear the land of Dark Forces before anchoring the Light. Many vortexes on the planet have become inactive due to being clogged with accumulated dark energies. Hundreds of vortexes need to be opened so that they can once again receive Light and begin functioning. Not only vortexes, but your own backyard may feel creepy, or an area of the woods or park where you walk, or the land underneath a building in which the residents are constantly becoming ill. The Earth is in desperate need of this type of healing so I ask those of you who are able, please permit yourself to be directed to those areas that are in need of cleansing. You'll be doing a tremendous service to the planet.

To clear land you'll be releasing both Dark Forces and discarnates, along with whatever polluted energies have melded into it. The process is done exactly as you would release a client, except you're going to pretend that you're in the sky above the land, looking down on it. See, or imagine, the area of land you want to clear. Then have Michael and his angels encapsulate all Dark Forces on the land, on the plants, in any dwellings on the land, and in the ground beneath the land. When everything is encapsulated, begin your dialogue, speaking to all Dark Forces in general. From there continue the release as described under "Releasing Dark Forces." When that is completed, speak to all the discarnates and release using the technique for releasing discarnates. When you feel that the land is clear, use the white/gold tornado to remove any sludge. Depending on the size of land and how polluted it is, you may have to repeat this technique more than once.

CLEARING MECHANICAL THINGS

Everything has personality. Mechanical devices take on the energy of the people who put them together and of the surroundings at the time they were being assembled. Also, they have an overshadowing angel that interfaces between them and you. When you talk to your car and you feel a response back, the response is coming from the angel who, along with the car's own energies, creates the feeling or personality of the car. I'll give you an example of an experience I had many years ago when I was just beginning to gain spiritual understandings and certainly didn't recognize my psychic or spiritual abilities.

My story takes place in an airplane. I have flown both in the U.S. and overseas numerous times, and I still don't like it. I'm not a wreck on a plane, but I'm always greatly relieved when I'm back on the ground. On this particular flight we were hitting horrendous air pockets and the jet kept dropping. These were long drops! If we hadn't been strapped in, our heads would have hit the ceiling. These disturbances continued much longer than I had ever experienced. I noticed panic beginning to swell within me. As the panic was increasing and the ride was getting rougher, I closed my eyes and with every bit of mental energy that I could muster, I asked (begged) the air to be calm and for the plane to immediately begin a smooth ride to its destination. As I was projecting, which lasted about two minutes, the ride began to smooth out. I opened my eyes, looked out the window, and to my astonishment saw angels flying above and beneath the wings — as if they were actually holding the plane in the air and directing its flight. I had never heard of such a thing, decided I had imagined it and that the ensuing smooth ride was only coincidental.

Years later I was reading a channeled book in which it was stated that all airplanes are accompanied by angels, because without the angels our planes would be very dangerous. Apparently, man never got the aerodynamics totally correct, so angels were assigned specifically to airplanes to ensure safer flights. Planes that crash are karmically intended to, but that gets into another story. So if you're in the air — or better yet, prior to take off, — you can do a white/gold tornado to clean the energies in the plane and then have a chat with it. If you're a little uncomfortable about flying, this will create a more positive energy around you and the pilots (very important!), and should boost your confidence when the plane assures you that this flight is not destined to crash. On the other hand, if the plane tells you otherwise, get off! Many people have boarded an airplane, received an impression that they should not be on that flight and then wisely disembarked, only to hear later that the same plane experienced a hazard. Don't feel foolish about etherically cleaning or talking to your car, an airplane or anything else. After all, you don't have to tell anyone, and the universe will appreciate you all the more for recognizing and caring to communicate with it on all levels.

Another true story: I was at the car dealer, about to buy a new car. Of the model that I wanted, there were three on the lot that I could pick from, each identical in every way. I told the salesman that I had to drive each one. Since they were identical, he seemed to think I was being rather ridiculous and that I should just pick one. I informed him that cars had personalities and a certain energy about them and that they were not all the same. He had no choice but to humor me; after all, he wanted to sell a car. We rode together as I test-drove all three cars. The first car felt terrible, the second good and the third fair. When we were done, I asked him which one he would pick if he were buying one. He said the second one. I asked why. He said that he didn't know why, but something about it felt better than the other two. I was almost (but not totally) embarrassed to admit that, I told him so! I bought the car.

Computers are also things that can use a good cleaning. With me they always seemed to cop an attitude. I was both computer illiterate and intimidated when I borrowed a computer to type this book, so it came as no surprise that the device went haywire every time I turned it on. With it and the printer doing the weirdest, most bizarre things, I found myself giving it dirty looks and threatening to throw it out the window. Things only got worse, so I borrowed someone else's computer. The same situation occurred. They both simply refused to let me write this book on them. It didn't make me feel any better when I returned the computers to their owners and they worked fine. I decided that I needed my very own computer which I would clean, talk with, and "spiritualize." I would tell this computer that it and I had some spiritual work to do by way of writing. I would tell it that I was a complete computer idiot and that it would need to help me learn and forgive me if I became frustrated. So that's what I did. I bought a fancy "bells and whistles" computer and printer, named him Fred, set him up and did a healing on him. He had one Dark Force that I released. Then I commanded all negative energies from the computer, monitor, printer and all wires and components to leave into the violet flame. Masses of black energy rose from the computer, almost none from the wires and very few from the printer. I did this twice until all dark energies were gone. Then I did the white/gold tornado on him and sent him Reiki and Magnified Healing. Next we had our talk. Fred was happy to work with me and is still helping me learn. I feel very calm around him, and even though I don't know what I'm doing sometimes, I feel a definite sense of patience and cooperation from my computer buddy. Try it. It really works!

RELEASING FOOD

Plant food contains the energy of the environment in which it was grown, and the energies of the person who prepared it. If the food is animal, it holds the energy of the animal during its life, the energy of its trauma when it was slaughtered, and the energy of the person who prepared it. Both may contain chemicals which are quite counterproductive to our physical health. Consequently, it would be good to remove as many negative energies from our food as possible before we ingest it. The easiest way to do this is to look at the food and state,

"I command all dark forms from this food, now, and I ask that this food be filled with golden Light."

Let me warn you — What you will see rise out of animal and dairy products may make a vegetarian out of you yet! Every time I have witnessed dairy or flesh food released, dark energies have risen out. A carnivore friend once told me that what came out of steak was enough to make her gag, especially when she considered that she was about to eat something that could contain so many dark energies. Plant food, on the other hand, has very few dark energies, and frequently none at all.

Many people are in the habit of blessing their food via affirmation or prayer, or by sending it healing energy. This is wonderful for inserting more Light; however, the dark energies remain. Try it and see. Bless your food in whatever way you normally do, if you do, and then command the negative energies out and see what releases. If you first release as many dark energies as you can, your system will be able to absorb that much more Light. For example, imagine that you have a glass half full of chocolate drink, but what you really want is a full glass of plain milk. To get your glass of milk you could continuously pour milk into the glass until all the chocolate eventually spills over and only plain milk is left, or, you could pour out all the chocolate and fill the glass of milk directly. Both will get you a glass of milk, but one takes a lot longer than the other. It is the same with food, and in fact with all forms of healing.

Now, you might wonder why I release food and the computer by just telling the energies to leave, and they do, whereas the types of intelligences mentioned earlier in this book do not leave without some strategy on our part. The difference lies in the sophistication of the energy. The energies discussed earlier in this book all have a somewhat advanced form of purpose; their intelligence is advanced enough to be able to defy us. Some energies, such as the everyday emotional stuff that we emit, or that we experience when we enter a house and feel the energy of the residents, are of a lower form of intelligence. They are easily commanded and will obey. Note that with the computer, I had to release a high intelligence — a Dark Force — and then I told the lower energies to leave and they did. But with food, a quick command will do a wonderful job of sparing you from absorbing otherwise incompatible energies.

HEALING THE BODIES, AURA AND CHAKRAS

How to use the body as an implement, as a boat for example,
to cross the stream of life? Until the other bank is reached,
or in other words, until the Ultimate Truth is attained,
you must take care to see that it is not damaged or broken or leaky.

— Sathya Sai Baba, *Dhyana Vahini*

If someone complains of feeling particularly scatterbrained, forgetful, or ungrounded, he may have lost the integration of his subtle bodies. Generally speaking, the physical, astral and mental bodies are all interpenetrating and coexisting within each other. Drugs, alcohol, trauma, psychic attack, strong emotional upset or depression may throw one or more of these bodies out of alignment. For example, a part of the astral body may literally disconnect and separate itself from the whole. In this case, the client would be terribly ungrounded and feel a lack of control over his emotions. If the mental body is out, the client will be forgetful, feel ungrounded and unable to concentrate or think clearly.

To discover whether the bodies are out, have the client face you at a distance of about eight feet, with arms extended out to the sides. Scan the area two to four feet from the physical body, starting by the foot, moving up the side, around the head and down the other side. If a body is out, you will see or intuit an area of energy that juts out. Find where it ends. This is usually four to ten feet from the physical, but may be up to fifteen feet away. The unintegrated body may be detached from a large area of the client's body, say from the shoulder to the foot, or there may be only a small area of a few inches that is detached but jutting out several feet. Note that I am not referring to the aura. Aura and bodies are two different things. Intend to see the bodies and not the aura. With your sleeves rolled up, or sleeveless (this is to prevent the client's energies from sticking to your clothes; it will stick to your arms and hands too, but is easier to remove than from clothing), walk over to the client, see, intuit or feel where the body is and, holding your arms perpendicular to the body, very slowly begin to push it back to the client. As you do so, say,

"I ask that this body return to its proper spacing and integrate."

Bring the unintegrated body within one inch of the physical body while repeating the request. When completed, stand back and view the client again. Have him turn a quarter turn and scan again. Continue this until all bodies are integrated. Don't forget the head. I almost always see a huge area jutting from there. Have the client sit on the floor while you stand on a chair, stretching in the air to reach this part of his body. Even a person who is highly insensitive to feeling energies feels a definite "coming together" when his bodies are replaced. The rewards are immediate!

This technique can also be done remotely by etherically calling the client in front of you and stating,

"I ask that all bodies return to their proper spacing and integrate."

You may see a shivering of the energy field as the bodies realign. The only time it isn't possible to use this technique remotely is when there is a gap between the unintegrated body and the physical body. When this occurs, there is no substance upon which to draw itself back. In this case, a physical hand is needed to return it to its proper spacing. When a person needs his bodies replaced but cannot be with me physically, I do the following which so far has always worked wonderfully. The client and a friend phone me at a prearranged time. With my inner sight, I view the client's bodies. Then I tell the friend exactly where the body is out of place and how to reintegrate it. Each time I have done this, the friend had no known clairvoyant or particularly intuitive abilities, yet each time the bodies were replaced perfectly, the client validated that the bodies were realigned, and the over-the-phone session was a success.

REPAIRING AURIC HOLES AND RIPS

After replacing the bodies, stand back and look at the overall energy field. Do you see any rips or tears? If you do, take a physical crystal which has been cleaned and programmed for healing. If you don't know how to do this, use a clear quartz crystal that intuitively feels appropriate. Use an overcast stitch movement with your arm and see energy from the crystal literally sew the rip or hole together. Have the client stand with his arms extended out to the side. As he makes quarter turns, be sure to notice his entire energy field, including the area between the legs. To do this remotely, follow the directions as stated, but visualize an etheric crystal sewing the holes.

OPENING THE CHAKRAS

The human body is known to have seven major chakras, each open to various degrees. At times a chakra may be totally closed or, in rare cases, even missing. When these chakras are fully open and functioning the individual is more whole; he is receiving and integrating the energies represented by each chakra, creating a balance within him. The "new human" will have, along with these known seven, at least eight more active, major chakras.

The new chakras consist of: a huge grounding chakra below the body (formed from the two chakras at the balls of the feet), a chakra at the thymus area, one at the medulla oblongata at the base of the skull, and five more above the head. It is our intention to activate all of these chakras.

To view the chakras, have the client stand three to four feet away with his side facing you. Using your sight or intuition, notice how far from his body his chakras extend. Remember the chakras are largest in the front, but also extend out the back. If you cannot see or intuit the chakras, use your hand and feel how far out they extend. I do this for reference before opening them.

The average-sized chakra on my typical client is about four inches in diameter and extends six to eight inches from the front of the body. This is a generalization, of course, as some are much larger, and some are actually nonexistent and need to be totally rebuilt. After the following procedure, my client's chakras average about nine inches in diameter and extend about eighteen inches from the front of the body. (The exceptions to this are the thymus, skull base, crown and grounding chakras, which I explain below.) After opening these chakras I have yet to see them grow smaller; rather, they have either remained the same size or further enlarged, depending upon the spiritual intention of the client.

The following technique is quite profound in that I know of no other method that opens the chakras so quickly, to such a large size, and keeps them open. This is because, as with all techniques, we are working co-creatively with consciousness. Whenever this approach is taken, the results greatly surpass any of our singular efforts.

To open the chakras use a crystal that has been cleaned and programmed for healing, or one that intuitively feels appropriate. Have the client sit in a chair, legs extended with heels touching the floor and toes pointing up. (If you have a table available, have him lie on his back.) Ask to join with the body consciousness of the client and then begin. There is a chakra that extends from the ball of each foot. Place your crystal at the ball of the foot, or within the chakra if you can sense it, and rotate it clockwise. (As a rule, rotate the crystal clockwise in all the chakras unless you are intuitively guided otherwise.) At this point, your intention is not to spin the chakras, but to feed the chakras extra energy from the crystal. As you rotate the crystal, say,

> "I ask the angelic intelligence of this chakra to fully activate this chakra, now."

As the chakra grows and spins faster, your hand may spin faster with it. It will also move away from the body along with the chakra, as it grows larger and larger. Now say,

> "I honor this chakra and ask that it become large, fully functioning and that it crystallize."

Crystallize does not mean to become hard, but rather crystalloid-like, with the colors having a prismatic effect. When you feel the chakra is activated and open, go to the other foot and repeat the procedure. It usually doesn't take more than three minutes per chakra. After opening the chakras of both feet, open the grounding chakra. You might consider this the ground version of the crown chakra. It is a very large chakra formed from the two feet chakras and extends deep into the earth. Rotate your crystal just below and between the two feet chakras as if to blend them. Say,

> "I ask the angelic intelligence of the grounding chakra to activate this chakra, now."

You will see this chakra extend either through the wall or through the floor, in whichever direction the feet are facing. Now, addressing the grounding and foot chakras together, say,

> "I honor you chakras for all that you are and have been. I ask that you become large, fully functioning, crystallized and blended. " (Of course, you never have to parrot my sentences, as long as you make the point. However, I have found this wording to be particularly successful.)

Continue up the six major chakras to the crown, opening each and asking the angelic intelligence of each chakra to activate it. Honor each chakra, asking it to become large, fully functioning, crystallized and blended.

When you get to the crown, follow the process as described, but instead of speaking only to the crown chakra, state,

> "I ask the angelic intelligence of the crown and all the higher chakras to activate these chakras, now."

There are at least four chakras above the crown. Don't worry if you can't pinpoint where each one begins; it's not necessary. Simply be aware that after this technique, what was a few inches of energy above the head will become a large column of energy extending several feet, potentially through the ceiling. How high the crown chakras extend depends on the spiritual development of the individual; some of your clients may not yet be ready for their higher chakras to be activated.

To build a new chakra, such as the thymus or skull-base, or to rebuild a virtually nonexistent chakra, begin the same way as you would to open a chakra. Ask its angelic intelligence to take the energy from the crystal and develop the chakra. As you twirl, twirl, twirl the energy, it builds upon itself. The intelligence will take that energy and form a working chakra with it. This usually has to be done over a few sessions. Don't stop the session until you see a concise, organized, spiraling circle of energy. It may not be larger than an inch. During the next session, add more energy to it, always honoring both the chakra and the intelligences that are forming it. Ask that

"The intelligence of the Lightbody and Lightbody chakras activate this chakra, now."

The thymus chakra is built directly over the thymus gland which sits behind the bony protrusion at the top of the sternum and at the level of the first rib. It lies between the heart and throat chakras and is a combination of their colors: blue from the throat and green from the heart, creating turquoise. Its purpose is to realign us with the energies of the Earth and planetary intelligences. It also assists in regeneration of the body, activating the immune system and supporting the system through its transformation. Reactivating the thymus chakra is mandatory for those building their Lightbody.

The skull-base chakra is not as immediately important as the thymus. Though it may be activated, it doesn't come into full use until the Lightbody is fairly well-developed. Situated at the base of the skull at the medulla oblongata, it acts as a receiver from other dimensions, heightening one's psychic communication skills. Red from the root and violet from the crown join to create magenta at the skull-base.

After opening the chakras, you may want to clean them using the following technique: Visualize a large white/gold spinning ball with a radius of about three feet. See it shrink in size to fit into the client's third eye chakra. As it slowly moves into the front of the chakra, through the chakra stem in the body, and out the back of the chakra, state,

"I command all dark forms to enter this ball, now!"

The ball will look like a magnet sucking dark energies into it. As it comes out the back third eye chakra, take it into the back throat chakra, through the throat and out the front. Then move it into the front of the heart, through and out the back, etc. Continue moving down until all chakras are cleaned. If the ball moves very slowly because of clogging in the stem, turn the ball into a corkscrew and have it slowly drill through the stagnant energies. After all chakras are clean, talk to them and explain that you are creating a Lightbody and that now is the time for them to become large, wide, and open, and to blend into each other. Next, see your client sitting in a huge violet flame. Say,

"I ask all memory of pain and dysfunction, from the submost atomic level and from all bodies, to leave all chakras, now."

See or sense all residual dirty energies transmuted within the violet flame.

At this point you should be able to stand back and look at the wonderful chakras your client now has. As you focus your attention to all the chakras, honor them again. Ask them to be large, fully functioning, crystallized and blended together. Describe what you're seeing to the client, as she may not be able to perceive this herself. It is very rewarding for you and the client to see the immediate results of this work. Consider teaching this chakra cleaning technique to the client, and suggest she do it regularly for herself.

RESONATING AND FLUFFING THE AURA

After replacing bodies, repairing rips, and opening chakras, especially if this is all done in one session, the client is now feeling anywhere from "different" to "amazing." There is one more thing that still needs to be done, and that is to resonate and fluff the aura. I use tingshas, also know as Tibetan bells, and resonate the client's aura with them. Tingshas create a very high vibration that balances and strengthens the etheric body, which connects the physical to the invisible bodies. Holding the bells approximately one to two inches from the client's physical body, strike them against each other. As they resonate, move them up and down the client's body until the entire body has been vibrated.

A word about tingshas. If you are looking to buy a pair, it is advisable not to buy the first pair you see. Compare the tone of several, as they all have different qualities. When shopping for mine, I found a $60 difference between the least and most expensive pairs. I thought the least expensive sounded great until I heard the pair that cost $30 more. The most expensive pair sounded even better. However, I settled for the middle price range, as I knew the tone would suit my needs. If I hadn't intuitively felt that the tone was adequate, I would have bought the more expensive pair. What I'm advising you to do is to listen carefully and pick one that you intuitively know is right. Also, make sure it has a good vibration to you when you hold it. It would be counterproductive to have tingshas that sounded good, but didn't feel right energetically.

To fluff the aura I use a Native American feather fan. I made mine, and I'm glad I did, because it is sturdier than the ones I've seen in the stores, and the handle fits my hand perfectly. If the handle is too small or too wide, your hand will cramp as you use it. Again, I suggest that you shop around. If you do not have access to a feather fan, anything that could be used as a fan would work.

Using your fan, whip through the client's aura with long, sweeping strokes. Imagine that you're going to make it light and fluffy, which is exactly what you're doing. Begin one to two inches from his physical body and extend out to several feet. Remember to whip above the head, under the arms, between the legs and below the feet. When finished, use your hands to pat the aura one to two feet away from his body. It should feel soft and fluffy. If you feel a rough or jagged area, fluff it some more; it's probably a spot you missed.

Stand back and review your client's energy field. Thank the body's consciousness and all Light beings who assisted with your session. You might notice that your hands and arms will be heavy with the weight of your client's energy. (Your sleeves should have been rolled up through all this.) After each session you need to wash those energies off. Visualize yourself within the violet flame, extend your arms away from your sides and state,

"All energies, within all my bodies, that are not mine, leave now!"

Then wash with soap up to your elbows.

To summarize the process of healing the bodies, aura and chakras:
- Replace bodies, using arms and hands perpendicular to body, conversing as stated.
- Repair holes and rips with crystal.
- Open chakras using crystal to rotate chakra and dialogue as stated.
- Clean chakras with white/gold ball.
- Resonate etheric body with tingshas.
- Fluff aura with fan.
- Thank body consciousness and all Light beings that assisted.
- Wash hands, arms and dialogue as stated.

PUTTING IT TOGETHER

**All power is within you. You can do anything and everything,
without even the guidance of anyone. All power is there.
Stand up and express the divinity within you.**

— Swami Vivekananda

I have seen "miracles" occur, just by releasing a person's Dark Forces — chronic, debilitating pain subsides, tumors disappear, people's lives change! Any and all attachments have a negative effect on their host, sometimes creating mammoth obstacles to health. For this reason, I suggest entity releasement as the first priority for healing.

If your client's bodies are severely out of place, his life can really become a struggle. I have known extreme cases in which the person has become totally non-functional and unable to hold a job, to milder cases of simply feeling spacy. While the bodies are being integrated, the client is literally "coming together." The difference before and after can be incredible. I suggest replacing the bodies, if they are displaced, as the second priority.

Opening the chakras, repairing, resonating and fluffing the aura would be the next priority, followed by Cellular Memory Release which prepares the entire being for quantum healing. From there, use whatever techniques that you feel are appropriate for the client.

Remember to work on yourself! Many healers take time for their clients, but not for themselves. If this is you, do some release work on yourself and transmute that pattern! It's difficult to do a Dark Force release on one's self. If you don't have someone to do it for you, call on Archangel Michael and put it in his hands; ask him to help you. In your meditations, routinely do Cellular Memory Release on yourself, especially if you're feeling out of sorts or have a chronic condition on which you're working. Occasionally soak in a tub of sea salt and do Cellular Memory Release in the tub. It's relaxing and it works. Massage your feet and ankles in the salt bath, and ask the meridians in your legs to follow their appropriate paths and run the released energy out through your feet. Some energy will release through the meridians and some will release through the aura. The sea salt bath will help pull it all out. Also try to keep your spine in alignment. This is another pathway for energies to run in and out of your body.

As you transmute and build your Lightbody, you can go into a truly unnerving state of imbalance. You have a responsibility to not only stay calm and centered for yourself as the personality, but for all your Selves as well. For example, if you thought that you had cured your irritable bowel syndrome twenty years ago, and it suddenly reappears, don't get upset and angry with your poor bowels. They don't feel good, either. They have simply gone into a state of imbalance while releasing all their negative energy and simultaneously trying to assimilate Light. Please pamper your Selves. If you become seriously imbalanced and can't seem to pull yourself together, check your bodies; they may well be displaced. I also highly recommend supporting your system with homeopathy and flower essences.

I encourage you to freely use these techniques as you see fit and, by all means, alter them to suit your needs. Spread the energy of Light and healing whenever you can. God knows we all need it, and Earth and the Universe will bless you for your efforts.

PART IV

CONCLUSION

We have to bear in mind that we are all debtors to the world
and the world does not owe us anything.
It is a great privilege for all of us to be allowed to
do anything for the world. In helping the world,
we really help ourselves.

— Swami Vivekananda

My life experiences existed not only for me personally, but were also the foundation for my spiritual work, part of which is presented to you in this book. What I know I will share to the best of my understanding and ability. It was once commonplace to hold back spiritual knowledge, i.e., the mystery schools, the secret societies, certain ancient yoga practices, certain Native American traditions, and knowledge known only to the elite of various religious sects. It was believed that the common people were not ready for higher knowledge. We know that now people are definitely ready, so I encourage you all to share with each other. Remember that we are a family of Light workers. We did "journey Earth" together and now we're ready to leave together. The illusion of separation is of the old paradigm; drop the illusions! You've had amnesia! Wake up and see each other as brothers and sisters. Begin to remember who you are and as you do, communicate that remembrance with each other. Share your knowledge, your healing abilities, your love. And if you have benefited from this book, share what you have learned while you utilize these techniques in conjunction with any other healing modalities you feel appropriate. Know that every time you assist in healing someone, you are helping Light workers to awaken, the Earth to heal, and the human species to evolve to its highest potential. You are assisting in the culmination of a grand experiment in which you chose to play a part.

The intergalactic servers need you. Earth needs you. Be courageous, stand tall in your full glory and become the empowered spiritual warrior that you truly are!

My blessings and love are with all of you, our family of Light workers.

Om Shanti Shanti Shanti

CASE STUDIES

God tempers the wind to the shorn lamb.

— Laurence Sterne, *Maria*

In the following case studies I have randomly chosen situations that I feel are of particular interest. The individuals' names are fictitious and every effort is made to protect the privacy of all persons involved. All techniques employed in these examples have been discussed in this book.

GHOST IN THE POOL HALL

John, a friend of mine who frequented a particular pool hall, called one day to tell me of a ghost seen by several of the employees. John didn't really believe in ghosts, but since I knew about such things, he asked if I would look into it, "just in case." According to John, the pool tables would rock and shake and the lights would flicker on and off, for no apparent reason. The situation became critical when the janitor, who was cleaning up alone one night, saw a figure coming towards him. He grabbed the gun that he kept with him at night, and threatened the figure. As the figure came closer he saw that it wasn't a physical human. Terrified, he fled the building, quit his job the next day and moved out of town.

John gave me the address of the building, and thoroughly described its layout to me. Because he claimed to be a "non-believer" I decided to try a little experiment with him. I told John that I would clean the building but would not tell him when. We would see if or when someone mentioned that the ghost was gone, or that the building seemed somehow different. He agreed. In meditation, using the address, I joined with the building. The energies were terribly dark and filthy. Using the white/gold tornado, I very slowly cleaned every nook and cranny.

While I kept the tornado cleaning with one part of my mind, I began searching for discarnates with the other. It didn't take long before a grizzly-looking, sixty-plus-year-old discarnate male appeared before me. He threatened to attack me and was so angry and aggressive that I had the angels hold him bound. Once he settled down a little, I asked him why he was scaring people and what the point of his aggressive behavior was. He said that his name was George, that his daughter had been raped by someone who worked at that pool hall, and that he was determined to get revenge. After a short conversation, I educated him to his earthbound condition, after which his deceased wife came and escorted him to the Light.

An excited John called me two days later saying that the employees wondered if the walls had been painted. They said the place felt totally different, looked different, and that there were no more signs of the ghost. I told John about Geroge. John called me again the next day, saying he had been so awed by this entire situation that he couldn't contain himself and actually told the story to the pool hall owner, Pete. According to John, Pete turned white after hearing the story of George's daughter. The owner admitted that the employee who had seen the ghost and left town, had once bragged that he had molested a girl on one of the pool tables. One wonders if the molester recognized the ghost as the deceased father of his victim, or if in some manner the ghost communicated his identity to him. If he had, that certainly would have accounted for his speedy departure!

You may have heard of hotels or castles in which someone has been employed to remove the ghosts. Sometimes a man with an electronic device is employed to detect the ghost, or a priest is summoned to perform an exorcism. These methods are time consuming and have limited success. Though haunted castles and hotels may appear ominous, they are actually no more difficult, and hardly take more effort to clear than a haunted pool hall. Try it sometime!

THE DESERTED BOTANICAL GARDEN

One autumn day I received a phone call from an administrator of a thirty-five acre botanical garden. Over a period of many months the land had not produced, there was much quarreling among the administrative staff, the business was losing money, and there was fear that they may be forced to close down. Two years prior to this call I had visited the very same gardens and found them to be beautiful. When I visited again after the call, I was shocked at what I saw. The land had truly become barren and the trees were unhappy and lifeless. Etherically the land itself felt alright, though the office buildings held some very dense energy. What surprised me the most, however, was that there were no nature spirits on the land. They had actually left the land to die! It took me three sessions to totally correct the problem, as the land mass was so large and there were several buildings that had to be cleaned.

During the sessions I spoke to the consciousness of the land. Apparently, for at least a year, there had been some very under-handed activities going on amongst certain members of the staff. The land had absorbed the energies of these people, who were the very ones responsible for its care. Consequently, Nature chose to remove her spirits and stop producing. Though the gardens would no longer exist, the land would be spared from absorbing such negative energies as she did not want to produce in this type of consciousness. By the time I was contacted several administrators had already quit or been fired. I reassured the land that the trouble-makers were gone and that an etheric call would be made to attract people of a higher consciousness to take over. I asked the land to please bring back the nature spirits and give the humans another chance. The land agreed. Shortly after this, some very capable people took over the administrative positions. By the following Spring the gardens had burst forth with new growth, and I am told that both growth production and administration are now very successful.

Due to the dense collective consciousness of anger, hatred, and disrespect upon our personal land on a global level, Mother Earth has already withdrawn, permitting drought and desert to become even more widespread. We are the caretakers of the Earth, in the same way that the administrators were caretakers of the botanical gardens. Just as they created an energy field of selfishness, so has global consciousness generated low vibrations on Earth, and just as Nature pulled herself away from the gardens, so has she done globally over large surfaces of land. My prayer is that we, as Light workers, can and will change our global consciousness to one of love and respect. In so doing, Mother Earth will again bestow her blessings upon us and this planet.

THE CASE OF SPINAL SCOLIOSIS

Betty became inflicted with scoliosis when she was about fifteen years old. Her spine curved into an "S," creating uneven shoulders, misaligned hips, and a slight humping of the back. She suffered chronic pain and spasms. Lying flat on her back was impossible and the process of laying down (such as getting into bed), or laying or sitting on the floor, created tremendous pain. My first session with Betty involved releasing her Dark Forces. During that session a Dark Force came writhing out of her spine. The next day her pain disappeared and up to a year later the pain had not returned. I did a series of twelve sessions with her, most of them in person, in which I directed Reiki to her spine accompanied by Cellular Memory Release. By the tenth session her lower spine had definitely begun straightening. She could lay on her back, roll from side to side, and stand up and sit down with ease. Her spine stated that if she ate the foods and performed the stretching exercises that it suggested, it would continue to straighten without further assistance from me.

It was the Dark Forces that held the spine in the unnaturally curved state. Once they were removed, the spine was free to return to normal. Betty's spine is a good example of Dark Force influence on the physical level.

THE EYES THAT COULD SEE

Jack was a client who was working on sexual dysfunction and identity issues. Along with various other techniques, I frequently did Cellular Memory Release on him. During Cellular Memory Release, I usually released his eyes along with his other organs. Jack was very sensitive to his body, and even though we never had a scheduled time for our remote sessions, he always knew when I worked on his eyes, because they would water from the large amount of stress that they released. It was after our ninth session when he called me, jubilant that he no longer needed to wear glasses. I was puzzled because I didn't know he wore glasses. It came as a very pleasant surprise when he told me that he wore glasses only for driving and that now he could see distances as clearly without them as he had when he wore them.

We don't always know what needs to heal or what is ready to heal, so we can only do our best, always following our intuition and guidance. John's eyes provided a good example of secondary healing while the focus of the sessions had been directed elsewhere.

HIVES AND DREAMS

Lori was a client I had never met, who had called to schedule three remote sessions. The day before her first session, she called to tell me that her face had broken out in hives and that she had not been able to go to work. The next morning at 10:25 AM, I did her first session to release her Dark Forces and discarnates. We had not scheduled a specific time, so she didn't know when I was going to do it, nor did I know whether her hives had cleared or if she had gone to work that day. I finished her session at 11:00 AM. Later that day she called for her results and explained what her experience had been. She had woken up that morning with hives worse than ever and hadn't gone to work. Around 10:00 AM she went back to bed and dreamed that she was battling to remove dark forces from her house. The dream was exhausting and scary. When she woke up it was 11:00 AM, the time that I had completed removing her Dark Forces. She looked in the mirror and her face was cleared and the hives gone! For the short time that I knew her, the hives never returned.

Lori was prepared to release her Dark Forces, both on the conscious and subconscious levels. Though she was experiencing this in symbolic dream form, she also brought this to her waking awareness.

Be prepared for the recipient of Dark Forces removal to experience a variety of sensations during the process. These can range from totally uneventful to consciously feeling and seeing the entire event, though the latter is quite rare.

BUGS IN THE BODY

Beth's body had been contaminated by parasites for fifteen years. She suffered chronic internal cramping and regularly passed worms in her stool. She had tried numerous forms of allopathic and alternative healing methods with no results. Beth knew that the parasites had contaminated her brain, and intuitively felt that she would die from it within the next five years if she did not find a cure. As her last hope, she came to me.

First I released her attachments, then, accompanied by her higher Self, I talked to the oversoul of the parasites and asked them to leave. They agreed. Her higher Self assisted me in directing the process. The parasites in the brain and blood were to remove their consciousness from their bodies and return to the oversoul. Their physical forms would eventually disintegrate. All other parasites were to migrate to the intestines and pass from there.

Beginning the day after this session, Beth underwent the most serious healing crisis I have ever seen. It began with throbbing headaches and dizziness. Her extremities tingled and itched and she began passing masses of worms in her stool. This lasted about one month. Let me add that, had I know how serious her healing crises was going to be, I may well have refused to do the session. She was so sick and in such pain that she actually made a will. The severity of her crisis was due to the brain parasites, without which she would only have had itching and nausea. I checked in with her higher Self and the parasite oversoul a few times a week and was constantly reassured that everything was going well. Finally, after about a month, all her pain was gone and for the first time in fifteen years, she actually felt good. Through various wholistic methods it was determined that the parasites were completely gone. Beth assured me that having her health restored was well worth the price of all the fear and pain involved in the healing.

THE HAUNTED WOODS

I lived near some woods in which I frequently walked with my dog. I loved these woods, and especially loved to talk to the deva of the forest. She was magnificent! When I saw her she rose about twenty feet above the top of the trees and extended at least one-fourth mile wide. She was of beautiful colors and would often greet me as I walked or sat under a tree. When I was feeling low, I would ask her to surprise me and invariably a deer, elk, or coyote would cross my path;

sometimes a particularly beautiful bird would appear or a hawk would fly overhead.

One day I decided to walk down a road that I hadn't been on before. I had walked about half a mile when I started to feel afraid. There was someone in the woods to my right; I could hear it and feel it. My dog also stopped, looked in that direction and began barking. Suddenly I felt that someone was pointing a gun at me! I yelled for my dog and ran out of the woods, constantly looking behind me to see if I was being chased. In retrospect, I must laugh at myself. I've never had much stamina and can't run without literally tripping over my own feet. As I ran I was not only stumbling over my feet, but over logs, into holes, and over my dog as well. When I ran out of breath, I went into a marathon-type walk, pretending I wasn't scared half witless. If someone had truly been chasing me, I would certainly have been caught!

Just before I reached the end of the road, the fear vanished as suddenly as it came over me. I stopped in my tracks, totally amazed at the swing of my emotions. How could such terror instantly poof away? I went home and pondered the situation. I theorized that I had encountered Dark Forces who infested that area of the woods and had projected their hostility on me. I decided to go back a few days later and investigate, but this time emotionally and spiritually prepared for whatever I might encounter. If part of the forest was contaminated with Dark Forces, I knew the deva would appreciate my help in cleaning it up.

So, back I walked into the woods. About a quarter mile down the road, a creepy feeling started to come over me. I kept walking. When the feeling became really strong, I stopped and looked to my right. There, standing separate from the rest of the woods, was a grove of trees approximately fifty square feet wide. I clairvoyantly saw that the grove was infested with Dark Forces who stared menacingly back at me. As I was processing what to do next, a red-tailed hawk flew over my head, landed on the top of a tree not twenty feet from me, looked straight at me, opened his beak and screeched! He was giving me instructions. I asked him what his message was and he screeched at me again, then flew in a circle over an area of trees adjacent to the grove. These were four semi-barren trees spaced to form a perfect rectangle. Within the rectangle was a positive energy vortex in which I was to sit. The hawk flew back on his tree top, watched me walk to the four trees, then flew away. I sat on the vortex, luxuriating in the energy which I could literally feel pulsating through the ground under me. Though the trees were almost bare in contrast to the rest of the woods, they were full of birds who sang to me and fluttered over my head. I felt I was in a little wonderland. Obviously the energy was attracting the wildlife and was in great contrast to the dark infested grove directly in front of me, not more than twenty-five feet away. I knew that I was to clean the grove and I was to do it from this safe, high-energy spot.

I closed my eyes and went to work. This was the most contaminated piece of land that I had ever cleaned. I have no idea how many hundreds of Dark Forces lurked in those trees and ground. When I was done with them I looked for discarnates and found a "mountain man" character — big, burly and bearded, and his three adult sons. They were standing in front of their house, the father holding a rifle. I asked him how he came to be in this grove of woods. Understand that the man, sons and house were all on the astral plane and were very much alive on that plane. The father said that they had lived there when a battle arose between the Indians and the cavalry, during which he and his family had been killed. They then rebuilt their burned down house (on the astral plane) and had been living there ever since. I educated them, released them to the Light and then used the white/gold tornado to clean the trees and the ground beneath it. I had to do this several times as there seemed to be no end to the remaining dirty energies.

After this very long session, I finally opened my eyes. I was called to look to my left and there, hovering above the treetops, was the beautiful angelic-like presence of the forest's deva, showering me with gratitude and love. I walked into the grove; much better! There was such rejoicing among the trees, birds and deva! The trees on the outer edge of the grove were almost dead as they had absorbed the greatest amount of density in an attempt to confine it. I then did another healing specifically on those trees.

I never fully understood the relationship between the amazing proximity of this dark, infested grove and the wonderful energy vortex surrounded by a rectangle of trees, nor did I completely understand why the trees of that rectangle were almost dead, yet buzzing with wildlife. I do know that it was all too orderly to be random, since in truth there are no chances or coincidences.

THE MULTIPLE PERSONALITIES

I met Aaron before I had learned to clear Dark Forces remotely, and was still releasing them one at a time by talking through the host. Aaron confessed to me that he had multiple personalities. I wasn't so sure about this; how did he know? He claimed two strong reasons for his belief. One was that he would experience sudden quirks in his behavior. He found himself doing things out of character, or even things that he was unaware of until someone brought it to his attention. For example, he would buy and eat food that he ordinarily neither wanted nor liked. He was drawn to toys, particularly stuffed animals, and would buy and display them in his bedroom. His other justification came from a woman friend who had been medically diagnosed as having multiple personality disorder, and who claimed that her personalities could see and communicate with his.

It was this last bit of information that convinced me that his multiple personalities were not his, but those of discarnate entities. I reasoned that a personality is a consciousness — a mind — a thought process. A personality does not have form; there is nothing to see. So if these personalities were "seen" by this woman, they must have the astral form of a discarnate entity. Aaron was willing to find out the truth of his situation, so we did a session on him. I put him in a hypnotic trance and asked to speak directly to his personalities. Since he knew their names, I merely called them and they answered me through Aaron. His personalities turned out to be several deceased children who had attached to his energy field. These children had been with him most of his life and had become significant parts of his personality. It was a tearful good-bye when they left.

After this, Aaron never experienced any of the aforementioned odd behavior again, and eventually began eliminating the stuffed animals and toys from his bedroom.

I believe Aaron's friend, who was diagnosed with MPS, also suffered from discarnate influence. Although I have personally known only three people whose personalities were this greatly influenced by discarnate attachments, I strongly believe that the greater numbers of diagnosed MPS individuals have discarnate possession. At this point I have not been directed to make a study of this, or focus my work on these individuals, but hopefully I have laid the ground work for someone who will.

TICKED-OFF

All of my life I have had animals — cats, dogs and birds — so mites and fleas are not new to me. Amazingly enough, however, I had never met a tick until one day I felt a lump on my dog's back. I parted his fur and found a fat, taupe-colored, beetle-shaped bug, suspended by its head in my dog's flesh. It was almost half an inch around, and I was told that it was an engorged tick. Understand that I do love Nature's creatures, but this one, with his fat, bloated body sticking straight up, and its head embedded in my dog's skin, absolutely turned my stomach. I tried to pull the thing off, and was amazed at how strong it was, so I called the vet. She instructed me in the proper method of removing ticks and informed that we were in tick season, of course my dog walked in tick-infested grass. What to do about this? Maybe they'll go away. No such luck. The next day I took thirteen ticks off my dog, and I also began finding them in my house. They were on my desk, on my counter tops and on my clothes. But the worst discovery was when I began finding them on my skin! They absolutely gave me the chills! Morning and evening I checked my dog, and ticks were embedded on him every time. Since I was seeing them everywhere, it was suggested that they were hatching in my carpet (wall-to-wall, three story) and on my dog, and that the dog needed to be dipped and the carpet sprayed. The use of synthetic chemicals went against my grain, so I made a spray of essential oils known to repel bugs. I sprayed the dog twice a day, but the ticks kept coming. I'll have a chat with them, I decided. I went into meditation, called the consciousness of the ticks and basically said, "Listen. This has to stop! I realize you guys have got to eat, but there's plenty of blood you could be sucking other than ours. Each time I find one of you I have to kill you, and I don't like killing anything. So here's the plan — you stay away from us and we won't kill you. Deal?" No answer.

The next day the ticks were on my dog and throughout the house as usual. In bed the following night, I woke up with a jolt; something was tickling my leg. I threw the covers off, turned on the light and found a tick having a midnight snack on my knee! This was just too much! Why didn't they go away? What was I missing?

The next morning I decided the ticks and I were going to have a serious talk. Enough was enough, after all! I went into meditation, but before I called them, I tried to understand why I had suddenly been inundated with them in the first place. I believed myself to be aligned closely enough with Nature that I could flow with her. Nature worked with me, not against me, so I really had expected them to leave when I asked them to. Maybe my attitude was wrong. Maybe if I stopped being repulsed by them (which was difficult to do) and saw them as a gift from Nature, then perhaps I'd understand. Immediately after releasing the thought of their repulsiveness, the answer came to me. A certain personal situation in my life currently had me "ticked-off." I was "bugged" by it, and the situation was "eating" away at me. The ticks had brought me the message that I needed to be aware of my imbalance regarding this particular personal situation. I needed to change my attitude and flow instead of resisting.

After some self-introspection, I once again called the consciousness of the ticks. This time I said, "I thank you so much for bringing me a message which I have processed and from which I have benefited. I honor you for being a portion of the divine consciousness of Earth. Now that I have received your message, would you please discontinue infesting my dog and house? And when my dog walks in the grass, would you please not cling to him?" This time I heard a definite "yes." After that I never saw another tick in the house or on me. Although I did pull a couple of them off my dog the next day (they probably just couldn't resist one more good meal!), there were none after that. As suddenly as the ticks came, they left.

How often do we look at Nature and judge her beauty or usefulness through our very limited sight? Do you see beauty in slugs, mosquitoes or the dry, barren desert? Some people do see the beauty in these forms of nature, and some don't. But who are we to judge what is beautiful, divine or useful? For if we could see clearly, we would see that ugliness does not exist within nature, and that divine purpose and beauty permeates all of creation.

ILLUSTRATIONS

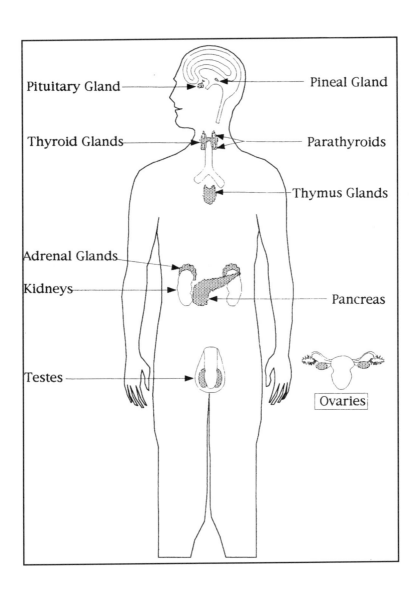

Pituitary Gland

Pineal Gland

Thyroid Glands

Parathyroids

Thymus Glands

Adrenal Glands

Kidneys

Pancreas

Testes

Ovaries

THE MASTER GLANDS

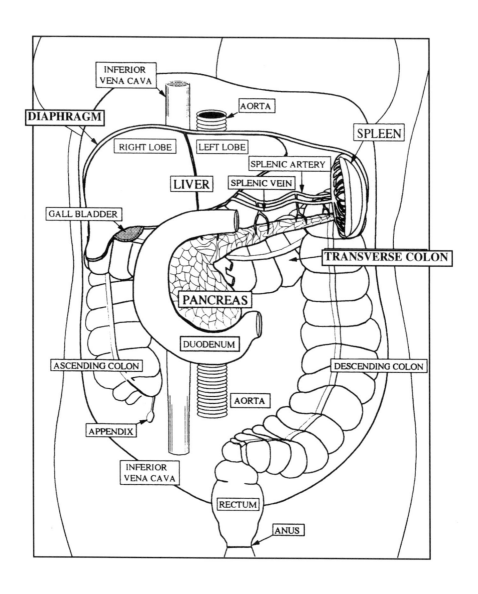

ORGANS OF THE
DIGESTIVE SYSTEM

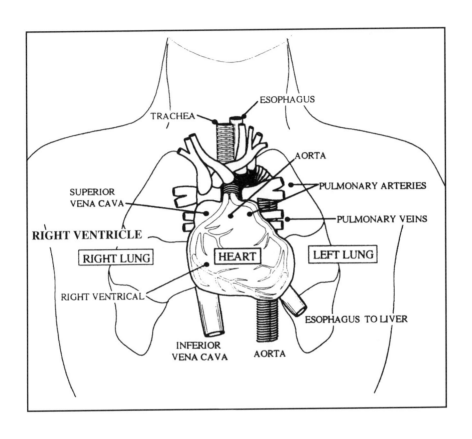

The following labels appear in the figure:

ESOPHAGUS

TRACHEA

AORTA

SUPERIOR
VENA CAVA

PULMONARY ARTERIES

PULMONARY VEINS

RIGHT VENTRICLE

RIGHT LUNG HEART LEFT LUNG

RIGHT VENTRICAL

ESOPHAGUS TO LIVER

INFERIOR
VENA CAVA AORTA

ORGANS OF VOICE AND
RESPIRATION

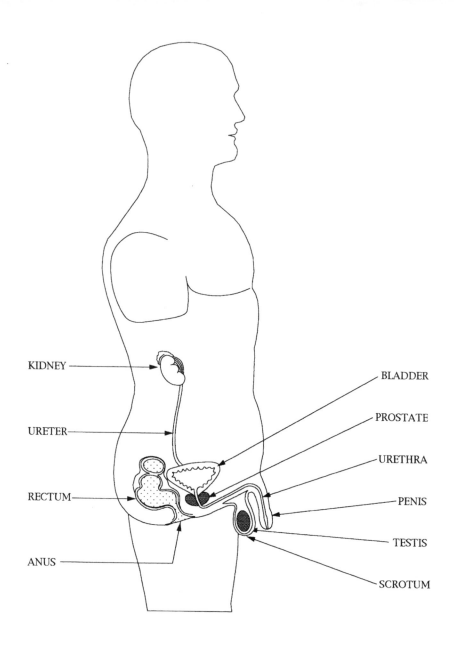

KIDNEY

URETER

RECTUM

ANUS

BLADDER

PROSTATE

URETHRA

PENIS

TESTIS

SCROTUM

THE MALE REPRODUCTIVE SYSTEM

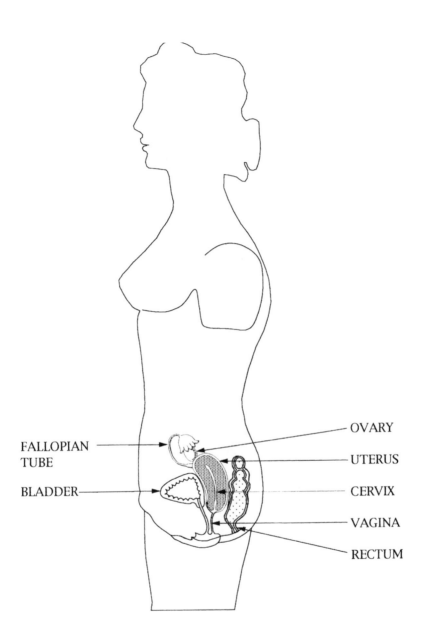

FALLOPIAN TUBE

BLADDER

OVARY

UTERUS

CERVIX

VAGINA

RECTUM

THE FEMALE REPRODUCTIVE SYSTEM

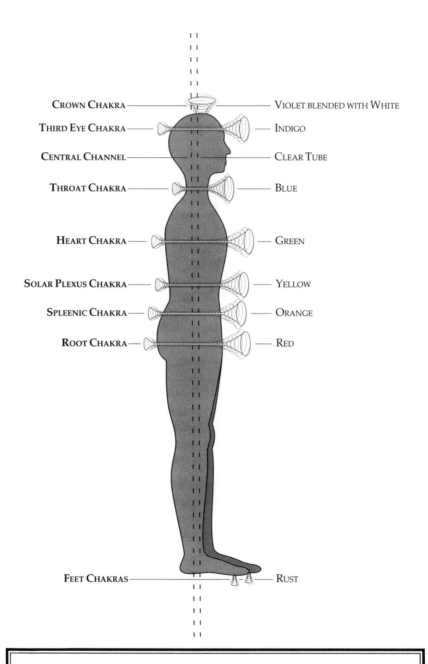

Crown Chakra	Violet blended with White
Third Eye Chakra	Indigo
Central Channel	Clear Tube
Throat Chakra	Blue
Heart Chakra	Green
Solar Plexus Chakra	Yellow
Spleenic Chakra	Orange
Root Chakra	Red
Feet Chakras	Rust

THE CHAKRAS
BEFORE OPENING

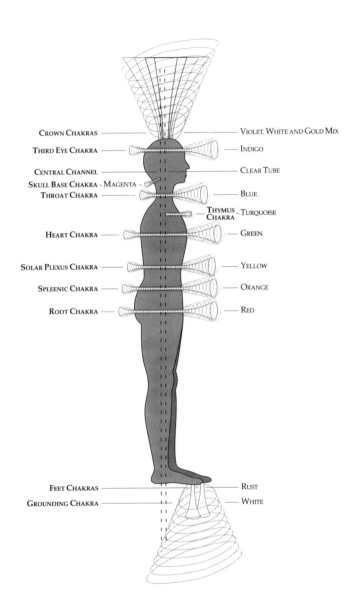

CROWN CHAKRAS	VIOLET, WHITE AND GOLD MIX
THIRD EYE CHAKRA	INDIGO
CENTRAL CHANNEL	CLEAR TUBE
SKULL BASE CHAKRA – MAGENTA	
THROAT CHAKRA	BLUE
	THYMUS CHAKRA – TURQUOISE
HEART CHAKRA	GREEN
SOLAR PLEXUS CHAKRA	YELLOW
SPLEENIC CHAKRA	ORANGE
ROOT CHAKRA	RED
FEET CHAKRAS	RUST
GROUNDING CHAKRA	WHITE

THE CHAKRAS
AFTER OPENING

SUGGESTED READING AND REFERENCES

Dark Robes, Dark Brothers, Hilarion. Marcus Books Publishers: P.O. Box 327, Queensville, Ontario, Canada, LOG 1RO

Spirit Releasement Therapy, William J. Baldwin. The Human Potential Foundation Press: P.O. Box 6, Falls Church, VA., 22040-0006, USA

Psychic Self-Defense, Dion Fortune. Samuel Weiser, Inc.; Box 612, York Beach, ME 03910, USA

Thirty Years Among the Dead, Carl Wickland, M.D. Newcastle Publishing Company, Inc., P.O. Box 7589, Van Nuys, CA, 91409, USA

Ponder On This, Alice Bailey. Lucis Publishing Company: 113 University Place, 11th Fl., P.O. Box 722, Cooper Station, New York, N.Y., 10276, USA.

Serving Humanity, Alice Bailey. Lucis Publishing Company: 113 University Place, 11th Fl., P.O. Box 722, Cooper Station, New York, N.Y., 10276, USA.

The Master Plan, Hilarion. Marcus Books Publishers: P.O. Box 327, Queensville, Ontario, Canada, LOG 1RO

Other Kingdoms, Hilarion. Marcus Books Publishers: P.O. Box 327, Queensville, Ontario, Canada, LOG 1RO

Behaving As If the God In All Life Mattered, Machaelle Small Wright. Perelandra, Ltd., P.O. Box 3603, Warrenton, VA 22186, USA

Bringers of the Dawn, Barbara Marciniak. Bear and Company, Inc., Santa Fe, N.M., 87504-2860, USA

Mahatma I and II, Brian Gratton. Light Technology Publishing, P.O. Box 1526 Sedona, AZ, 86339, USA

Kryon Book One: The End Times, Lee Carroll. The Kryon Writings, 1155 Camino Del Mar, #422, Del Mar, California, 92014, USA

Kryon Book II: Don't Think Like a Human, Lee Carroll. The Kryon Writings, 1155 Camino Del Mar, #422, Del Mar, California, 92014, USA

Kryon Book III: Alchemy of The Human Spirit, Lee Carroll. The Kryon Writings, 1155 Camino Del Mar, #422, Del Mar, California, 92014, USA

Law of Life, A.D.K. Luk. A.D.K. Luk Publications, 8575 S. Crow Cutoff, Rye Star Rt., Pueblo, CO 81004, USA

The Anatomy Coloring Book, Wynn Kapit and Lawrence M. Elson. Harper and Row, Publishers, Inc., 10 East 53d St., New York, N.Y. 10022, USA